I0199729

"In this beautiful and deeply personal set of reflections, Rabbi Anson Laytner not only does theology but offers us a model for how best to do it: with deep honesty and genuine humility. Rabbi Laytner shares his own journey through suffering and devastation in the hopes, I think, of illuminating and giving us courage to face our own. This is a book to be read slowly and savored, a spiritual testament from a rabbi and teacher who is, first and last, a seeker."

—SHAI HELD,
president and dean, The Hadar Institute; author of *The Heart of Torah*

"With a rare combination of head and heart, Anson Laytner shares his struggle to make meaning out of both the Holocaust and the series of blows his family suffered. Eschewing traditional answers, he grounds his hard-won theological reflections in experience, pursuing a life-giving meaning with passion and integrity. Along the way he takes the reader on a spiritual journey from grief to protest to compassion and acceptance. To accompany him is a blessing."

—MARY LANE POTTER,
author of *Strangers and Sojourners*

"Rabbi Laytner approaches the problem of suffering with refreshingly personal and raw candor. As a pioneering scholar of the Jewish tradition of arguing with God, Laytner knows both the spiritual benefits and limits of expressing authentic anger in prayer. Whether it be discovering the Dao of Torah, hearing a personally transformative message in a Bob Marley song, or even fainting in synagogue, Laytner's journey compels us to reflect on our own spirituality with naked honesty."

—DANIEL DEFOREST LONDON,
author of *Theodicy and Spirituality in the Fourth Gospel*

"Rabbi Laytner writes, 'All theology is personal.' That's true because all suffering is personal, and without suffering we'd give no thought to God. But what if you could go beyond the personal? What if you could experience a Greater Reality that embraces and transcends the personal? What if God knew you because God was you? Bring these questions to Rabbi Laytner's marvelous book, *Choosing Life after Tragedy*, and the answers you receive with astound you."

—RAMI SHAPIRO,
author of *Judaism without Tribalism*

Choosing Life after Tragedy

Choosing Life after Tragedy

An Experience-Based Theological Journey

ANSON HUGH LAYTNER

RESOURCE *Publications* · Eugene, Oregon

CHOOSING LIFE AFTER TRAGEDY
An Experience-Based Theological Journey

Copyright © 2023 Anson Hugh Laytner. All rights reserved. Except for brief quotations in critical publications or reviews, no part of this book may be reproduced in any manner without prior written permission from the publisher. Write: Permissions, Wipf and Stock Publishers, 199 W. 8th Ave., Suite 3, Eugene, OR 97401.

Resource Publications
An Imprint of Wipf and Stock Publishers
199 W. 8th Ave., Suite 3
Eugene, OR 97401

www.wipfandstock.com

PAPERBACK ISBN: 978-1-6667-7048-3
HARDCOVER ISBN: 978-1-6667-7049-0
EBOOK ISBN: 978-1-6667-7050-6

05/05/23

The author and publisher gratefully acknowledge the following for their permission to reprint material found in this book:

Excerpt from p. 182 from *Letters from the Earth by Mark Twain*, edited by Bernard DeVoto. Copyright 1938, 1944, 1946, 1959, 1962 by The Mark Twain Company. Copyright ©1942 by The President and Fellows of Harvard College. Reprinted by permission of HarperCollins Publishers.

Friedrich Torberg's poem, "Seder, 1944," in *Voices within the Ark: The Modern Jewish Poets,* Howard Schwartz and Anthony Rudolph, eds. Copyright ©1980 by Avon Books. Reprinted by permission of the Estate of Erna Rosenfeld.

The following essays of mine explored many of the ideas and material now found in this book:

"A Healing Process in Jewish Theology: From Passivity to Protest to Peace," in *Loss and Hope: Global, Interreligious and Interdisciplinary Perspectives.* Peter Admirand, ed. London: Bloomsbury, 2014. Used with permission.

"Jewish Leadership for Interreligious Dialogue," in *Religious Leadership: A Reference Handbook*, vol 2. Sharon Henderson Callahan, ed. Los Angeles: SAGE Reference, 2013. Used with permission.

"Jews, God and Theodicy," in *Religious Identity and Renewal: Jewish, Christian and Muslim Explorations.* Simone Sinn and Michael Reid Trice, eds. Leipzig: Evangelishce Verlagsanstalt, 2015. Used with permission.

To my family of survivors: Richelle; Michael, Jackson and Nico; Anna, Daryl, Gaby and Jacob; Miryam, Mark and Ari.

I can live with doubt and uncertainty
and not knowing.
I think it's much more interesting to live
not knowing
than to have answers which might be wrong.

—RICHARD P. FEYNMAN, PHYSICIST

Be sure that every deed counts, that every word is power,
and that we all can do our share to redeem the world
in spite of all absurdities and all frustrations and all
disappointments. . .
Remember the importance of self-discipline, study the great
sources of wisdom. . .
Above all, remember. . .to build a life as if it were a work of art.

—ABRAHAM JOSHUA HESCHEL, RABBI AND ACTIVIST

Contents

Acknowledgments

A SPECIAL THANKS TO Bonnie Fetterman, Mary Jane Francis, Richard Gordon and the late Jordan Paper for their detailed comments and insights on this manuscript, and also to these family members, friends, and colleagues for sharing their thoughts with me over these many years: Rich Agler, David Blumenthal, Dan Bridge, Shoshana Brown, Dorothy Bullitt, Deborah Cohen, Charles Davis, Atta Dawahare, Gene Duvernoy, James Eblen, Sol Ezekiel, Andrew Fenniman, Charlie Freedenberg, Abby Grasek, Joyce Greenberg, Richelle Harrell, Lesley Hazelton, Adrian Hill, Bruce Hosford, Bruce Kochis, Trudy James, Debra Jarvis, Anya Johnson, Tammy Kaiser, Michael Kinnamon, Merrily Laytner, Phil Levine, Suzi LeVine, Hubert Locke, Wayne Lubin, Barb Maduell, Marla Meislin, Jed Myers, Daniel Migliore, Ruth Morris, Marsha Olsen, Janet Parker, Julie Pfau, Judy Pigott, Kathryn Robinson, Stan Rosen, Judith Sanderson, Lee Seese, Ed Shields, Michael Trice, Helen Vandeman, Jane White Vulliet, and Elizabeth Wales.

Chapter 1

In the Beginning

EACH OF US HAS a life story, a spiritual journey, something that we may return to time and time again as we age, and this book represents a significant portion of mine. Only a portion because, first of all, I'm not dead yet so the story remains unfinished, and second, because as long as I am alive I am constantly reflecting upon and reinterpreting my story to better fit into my understanding of what past experiences mean in the context of my life in the present.

At the heart of my story is a period of ten years during which my family and I endured wave after wave of suffering, grief and death. But at the same time, it is also a story filled with love and transformation. Although I hated much of the experience while living it, I now also embrace it because it made me who I am today.

This book explores how I struggled with the issue of why bad things happen to basically good people, a topic known in the theological trade as "theodicy"; how I dealt with spiritual/emotional crises while I and my family braved many waves of illness and death; how I left old beliefs behind and began developing new ones that better addressed the experiences I'd had.

I share my story and reflections with you, not because I am a paragon of faith, but in the hope that the wisdom I have acquired as a result of this dark encounter may be of benefit to you as well.

I try to do theology in a creative way, the way artists and poets and authors do their work. Were I a more gifted writer, I might have tried my hand at fiction in order to express my ideas through the characters and events of a novel. My creative way to do theology is to make an explicit connection between my ideas, the work that I did, and my life story.

I believe that all theology is personal. By this I mean that there are complex personal factors that provide the shifting sands upon which any theology is built. But just as politicians prefer to obfuscate the personal motives underlying their decisions with grandiloquent rhetoric, so too do theologians generally cloak the personal roots of their theologies with dubious certainties. Instead, I try to keep my theology personal and rooted in my experiences.

For this reason, I use a number of autobiographical episodes to provide a loose narrative framework for this book. These experiences remain important to me because they were life-changing in some way. I offer you these portions of my life's journey to date simply as a sort of witness to the spiritual life and struggles of one thoughtful but otherwise ordinary fellow human being.

As I said at the very beginning, this book is my attempt to make sense of those recurring waves of disease, dying and death that washed over me and my family, leaving us gasping for meaning and dazed with pain. Of course, our family's experience is not unique. Other people have had life's events hit them far worse and I almost feel guilty about *kvetching* (complaining) about what we've gone through. Perhaps our experience is more compact and intense than that of other folk, but it is not so special.

Death, as it is so often blandly asserted, is just a part of life. As are pain and suffering. And happiness and joy too—but who complains about these? In truth, words cannot begin to convey the depth of feeling one has when in the thick of things, or the dark thoughts that these sorts of experiences can engender: "Why me?" "Why her?" "Why is God doing this to us?" "What did we do to deserve this?" "Why go on living?"

These are the kinds of questions that suffering raises for many people. They can haunt one's nights, sliding into one's consciousness between the ticks of the clock in the wee early hours, awakening us with an ache in the stomach, or with a troubling dream, or in an anxious sweat. Many people prefer, I think, to go for years without truly contemplating these questions, only to be violently confronted by them at a time of crisis and loss. At one time or another, though, all us are compelled by life's events to struggle to find meaning in what life throws our way, for better or for worse. We do so when we marvel at a birth or wonder about love, when we rage against disease or grieve over our dead.

These questions came to a personal head as I tried to make sense of the suffering my family had endured. What meaning is there in suffering, and how does it connect with God? For someone else, it might have been quite logical to ask, "Why believe in God in the first place, and even more so given all that suffering your family had gone through?" But for me, this was never an option. I knew there was a God. And the reason for my certainty was an experience I had had many decades earlier. . .

Chapter 2

I Experience "God"

I WAS JUST A *young man, in my late adolescence, still living in my parents' home, when I had my first taste of what I called "the divine." It was a summer's day, in the afternoon, and I was hiking in the ravine that lay below our home. Birds were singing, insects were flying about, the sun was shining, and a gentle breeze made the tree leaves shimmer with light. It was, in all respects, a normal summer's day. But as I walked along, I suddenly became aware of everything altogether: the birds, the insects, the trees, the stream, the earth, the air and me. We were one; or rather, everything I normally experienced as being outside myself, together with a sense of experiencing myself outside of myself—a sort of out of body sensation—were part of some whole Oneness. Initially, I felt myself lose significance and blend into my surroundings. Then I seemed to shrink in size as my perspective drew me further and further away from where I stood on the earth's surface. Finally, even as I felt myself merging deliciously into this Whole, I felt the sun's rays falling upon my head and shoulders, and just as suddenly as I had felt this sweet sensation of oneness—and yet without losing any of this sensation—I now felt a profound sense of my own uniqueness. The sun's rays were kissing me, only me, the only me that ever was or will be. I was at once part of and at one with all creation, yet simultaneously a unique and distinct* being. *I felt love and peace and joy. I was totally, wholly tranquil. And then the sensation passed. I walked on in a "holy" daze.*

I called what I had experienced "becoming aware of God." Why did I call it "God"? I called it "God" because it felt right to do so—although I certainly wasn't associating my experience with all that God has come to mean. From my encounter, I just knew that "God"—"Something Greater"—is present in our world, and that this "Presence" "is" "good"—how else could I interpret being bathed in the paradoxical but intensely beautiful sense of unity and uniqueness I had felt?

Years later, I learned a Hasidic saying that said that a person should go through life as if wearing a coat with two pockets. Each pocket contains a message. In one pocket are written the words "For my sake, the world was created"; and in the other pocket the words "I am but dust and ashes." One's life, therefore, ought to be a balancing act between these two standards of self-perception.[1] I wear that coat with its pockets of finite individuality and infinite unity!

What I had experienced was unlike anything I had ever learned about God in Jewish school or in formal prayer. Spirituality and the mystical experience were not exactly the coin in trade of the Canadian Reform Jewish congregation in which I grew up and was educated, nor was it part of my family's religious vocabulary. How did my experience connect with what my faith tradition taught? How did it relate to the experience of my people? So began my adult Jewish learning.

Along the way, I found another teaching that touched me profoundly. Yisrael ben Eliezer, the Baal Shem Tov, the eighteenth century European Jewish mystic who founded the Hasidic movement, taught that there are two reasons why many of the Jewish liturgy's basic prayers begin with the words "Our God and God of our ancestors." The first: that there are two ways of knowing God—through personal experience (our God) and through inherited tradition (God of our ancestors). The second: that the two are linked together as one so that we know that our personal and individual experiences of God are integrally connected to that which our ancestors also experienced. To better understand how Jews in ages past had experienced God then became my objective.

---

1. The Hasidic *rebbe* Simcha Bunim of Peshischa, d. 1827.

On my own and at York University in Toronto in the early 1970s, I began to study and contemplate the sacred texts of Judaism: the Tanakh (the Jewish Bible[2]), first and foremost; and also the teachings of the Rabbis found in the Midrash and Talmud. I also began to learn about Christianity and Islam and Baha'i; Hinduism, Buddhism and Daoism; and the latter two's offspring, Zen Buddhism. I also studied philosophers of the so-called Enlightenment period, the European skeptical tradition, and humanism. Then I returned to re-examine my own faith's teachings in the light of all I had studied. Ultimately, I decided to become a rabbi, not from a desire to serve a congregation but from a desire to learn and to have an opportunity for deep, spiritual growth.

A theological contradiction emerged almost immediately as I began my studies. According to Jewish tradition, "God" is an active deity, one who intervenes in history, a redeemer of the downtrodden, a giver of instruction, an upholder of justice and mercy. But what about the Holocaust? Why did God save the Children of Yisrael from Egyptian bondage yet do nothing to rescue this same people from Nazi savagery? Why those and not these? Why them and not us? And the more I pondered these kinds of questions, the greater the dissonance between my personal experience and the historical experience of my ancestors. What could I make of my experience of "God" considering the contradiction between the God of the Exodus and the God of Auschwitz? What did my sugarcoated experience of a beneficent and somehow sentient Presence have to do with the muck of human history and an absent or apathetic God? My once-splendid connection with the divine grew clouded and dim.

Yet certain stories captivated me from the get-go: Avraham (Abraham) rebuking God for His planned destruction of Sodom and Gomorrah; Ya'akov (Jacob) wresting the name "Yisra'el"—he who struggles with God—from a mysterious stranger after a nightlong fight; Moshe (Moses) vociferously arguing with God on behalf

---

2. Tanakh is a Hebrew abbreviation for the order of books in the Jewish Bible: Torah (Pentateuch), Nevi'im (Prophets) and Ketuvim (Writings). The Christian Old Testament orders them Torah, Writings, Prophets so that the latter's prophecies lead directly into the New Testament.

of the people Yisrael (Israel); Iyov (Job) fearlessly and defiantly pro-claiming his innocence. Here, I thought, was something unusual: people calling God to account, challenging God to abide by the same rules as God expected them to observe. These accounts spoke to my still adolescent soul and seemed to resolve my theological dilemma. I came to find my place with the God of my ancestors, but not with those who piously prayed, "On account of our sins are we punished . . ." rather with those who had called God to task for apparent indifference and inactivity in the face of perceived injus-tice. They gave God no peace and were not any more peaceful than I when faced with apparent divine inactivity. Their God became mine and I became another link in their defiant chain of protest. And perhaps this too was what the Baal Shem Tov had meant.

Chapter 3

China, Israel, America

AT YORK UNIVERSITY, I had ended up majoring in Chinese Studies, an odd choice for someone interested in the rabbinate, and one that I had more or less stumbled into in my intellectual wanderings. (To this day, I thank my parents for letting me follow my interests wherever they led without pressuring me regarding a future career.) In 1973, as I was about to graduate, I applied to a rabbinical school, the Hebrew Union College, so that I could continue my Jewish studies. My intention was either to become a Hillel rabbi working with university students or a professor of Jewish Studies. Then life intervened—China and Canada had just established diplomatic relations and I was offered the opportunity to study in China on the first Canada-China student exchange program. My professors urged me to apply; I did and soon was off to Beijing for a year. I deferred entry into rabbinical seminary until my return.

Although by no stretch of the imagination a spiritual experience, my year in Beijing was certainly transformative in many other ways. I left Canada as a thoroughly middle class, rather sheltered young man, still somewhat of a hippy and, like many university students at the time, fascinated by what we saw taking place in China, with the Red Guard, the Cultural Revolution and all that. At my school, the Beijing Language Institute, I met students from many other countries: I met my first Palestinians there, and other Arabs too; also, many Africans and Asians, and Europeans as well. Their life experiences opened my eyes to the larger world. So did China itself, then still a "Third World" country emerging from the self-inflicted ravages of the Cultural Revolution.

During my year in Beijing, I witnessed some of the final shudders of the "Great Cultural Revolution"—campaigns to criticize Lin Biao and Confucius, to criticize the Italian filmmaker Antonioni for his film on China, to criticize music without titles (like Beethoven's symphonies); each one accompanied by compulsory demonstrations, mandatory mass meetings, big character posters and fierce denunciations. Our Chinese colleagues did what they were told or had to face the consequences. I went to China rather enamored of its ideology and accomplishments; I left with a healthy aversion to the Communist system after observing how it attempted to control the lives of its citizens—and us as well.

While all this had a huge impact on me, it was my experience as a Jew there that really helped shape my future. Being in China, oddly enough, was a huge affirmation of my identity as a Jew. At first, I would introduce myself as a Canadian but, with my black curly hair and olive complexion, I would always be asked "But where did your people come from?" Apparently, I didn't look "Canadian" (whatever that is) and, since I knew I didn't exactly look Polish either, I said "Jewish." That satisfied everyone. As a Jew, I was just one of many nationalities in our school and it felt empowering to be one of the many minorities there. We were all equally odd in the sight of the Han majority population.

I found out to my surprise that people from Africa and Asia knew next to nothing about Jews and Judaism, Zionism and Israel, subjects near and dear to my heart. Often I was asked, "What did the Jews do that the Germans wanted to wipe them out?" It's a logical question—as if racism and anti-Semitism were logical phenomenon. But that was if they *even* knew about the Holocaust! Many Asians and Africans had not heard of it, and many had not even heard of the Bible, let alone read any of it. As a result of my experiences in China, I resolved that I would still become a rabbi but that I would use my knowledge to educate people in Africa and Asia about my people, its history and culture.

While in China, I also tried to visit the city of Kaifeng, home to the more-or-less indigenous Jews of China. Over a thousand years ago Jewish merchants had made their way to Kaifeng from Persia, both via the ocean and over the Silk Route, settled in this ancient capital city, built a synagogue, and flourished until the early nineteenth century. Even though the synagogue was long gone, reports indicated that members of this erstwhile community survived, and I resolved to visit Kaifeng when in China. Unfortunately, the city was still closed to foreigners on account of the Cultural Revolution, so I didn't get the chance to go there until some thirty years later. But the Kaifeng Jewish community remained an abiding interest of mine, leading to my involvement with the Sino-Judaic Institute and ultimately helping to shape my approach to God and Jewish tradition.

After a year in China, I went to Israel to begin rabbinical seminary. All Hebrew Union College rabbinical students spend their first year in Israel. This being 1974, a time when few Westerners, let alone Israeli Jews, had visited China, I found that my experience there gave me a key to the country. In Israel, everyone wanted to talk with me about my experiences. I met with someone from the Prime Minister's office and another from the Foreign Ministry, I spoke at various universities and at kibbutz centers, and I met Israeli and Palestinian peace activists. (This was at a time when collaboration was the norm not the exception.) Being in Israel and feeling myself a member of the Jewish nation and part of the majority population for the first time in my life was exhilarating. I almost ended up staying there. But common sense—and love in the form of a female rabbinic student—intervened, and I came to America on a student visa to continue my rabbinic studies in Cincinnati.

At the Hebrew Union College in Cincinnati, as I did research for my rabbinical thesis under the gruff guidance of Dr. Jakob Petuchowski, I gradually uncovered what I came to call "the Jewish tradition of arguing with God," a continuous line of protest that began with the first Jew, Avraham, and stretches down to our own day in the post-Holocaust works of various authors and poets, Elie Wiesel, Jacob Glatstein and others. I came to realize that the contradiction I experienced between God's saving acts of the past and

God's un-involvement in the present also had been felt by other Jews in prior generations: those who had experienced the destruction of the First or Second Temple, or had endured Roman persecution or the Crusades, or the Expulsion from Spain, or the pogroms in Eastern Europe, or the Holocaust.

My studies deeply affected my chosen career. I was theologically committed to "arguing with God" and dismissive of those who did not feel as I did. I denigrated congregational rabbis as mere "custodians of Jewish heritage" whose job it was to polish the artifacts, maintain the facilities and ensure access to Jewish tradition. In contrast, I saw myself as a "physician of the soul," and my task to diagnose the malady that afflicted my "patients." The illness I saw was the issue of theodicy and the cure was for people to offer prayers of protest voicing their anger about the Holocaust and their personal tragedies. Mine was a higher calling than simply providing solace. *They*—other rabbis—merely provided a bandage for the wound; *I* would treat the infection itself to offer a real healing. Paradoxically, I felt I could never work with people in crisis because I believed that the medicine I had to offer was not what they wanted—*even if* I knew it was what they needed.

But there was more to it than that. I also knew that I was avoiding the pastoral component of the rabbinate because I was afraid to experience people in their times of crisis. As a young man, I felt I lacked the personal wisdom, experience, and an appropriate theology to accompany people in their life journeys. Unlike my fellow rabbinical students who took on pastoral work even if they felt as I did, I was unwilling—and perhaps unable—to transcend my self-perceived inadequacies in the pastoral field.

Ultimately my career path centered on work in the non-profit sector, but I developed an avocation as an advocate for the "arguing with God" tradition and a teacher/lecturer on the subject. I lived for the opportunity to share my "discovery" of this tradition with as many people as possible.

As a rabbi, I felt I *had* to teach people what I had learned about this "hidden tradition" because I *knew* that it contained a measure of healing for the hurt of the Holocaust, which so many Jews continue to feel. And I was right. The subject matter electrified Jewish audiences. People thanked me for speaking about something they had had locked up in their hearts, for talking about a subject their own rabbis had been unwilling or unable to address, for reconnecting them with God and prayer again in a way that did not invalidate their own life experiences.

Chapter 4

Wave After Wave: Tragedy Strikes My Family

AFTER I GRADUATED FROM rabbinical school in 1979, my then-wife and I moved to the New York City area. I thought that being there would be a golden opportunity for me to begin a career in Jewish-Third World relations. To my utter surprise, the issue was no one's priority other than my own. None of the Jewish organizations headquartered there was interested, pre-occupied as they were with saving Soviet Jewry and defending Israel. Led by China, the "Third World" at that time was implacably hostile to Israel and Zionism—which made the national Jewish organizations shun outreach efforts to them even as my experiences in China had made such work irresistible to me. While I vainly looked for work in my chosen field, I continued researching and writing what became my first book, *Arguing with God: A Jewish Tradition.*

After three years in New York, my career took us to Seattle where I became the first full-time community relations director for the Jewish Federation of Greater Seattle. We had a daughter and later got divorced. I eventually remarried and added two teenage stepdaughters to my own five-year-old in a blended family. For twelve years things were mostly fine but then our safe little world began to crumble. . .

In the spring of 1999, my wife's brother, Michael, a man in his mid-sixties, died rather suddenly of bone cancer. On my family's side,

I lost an aunt in the summer and an uncle in the fall. That same autumn, my wife Merrily, then in her mid-fifties, was diagnosed with ovarian cancer and then, two days later, her sister, Jane, was diagnosed with an inoperable brain tumor. My wife had surgery and then spent the next six months in chemotherapy; her sister died within six weeks, sliding out of this world as she slipped deeper into sleep. She was sixty-three years of age.

The day we buried my sister-in-law, my mother, back in my hometown of Toronto, was admitted to a hospital suffering from heart failure. With the help of a pacemaker she recovered, but four days before the year's end, my father dropped dead, felled by a massive heart attack. To say that we were reeling from shock is an understatement. And then, just to make sure I truly comprehended my Job-like situation, I slipped on some ice, deeply bruising my lower back and, just as I was able to stand again, I got a bad case of shingles at the same latitude.

In early 2000, I was given a three-month sabbatical to mark my wife's completion of her chemo treatment and her return to health. The plan was that we would travel to Paris where we would celebrate her escape from cancer by enjoying the sites and, coincidently, I would work on a book on the meaning of suffering. Instead, life intervened. Our eldest daughter, Amy, at the time a vital and vibrant thirty-year-old woman with a one and a half-year-old son and a husband, was diagnosed with acute myelogenous leukemia. She spent the next three months receiving and then recuperating from intensive chemotherapy, including an entire month in the hospital. We "inherited" a very distraught and confused little grandson, who came to live with us, and still later, our daughter and her husband joined their son at our house for several months.

But while Amy was receiving chemotherapy, I had to rush to Toronto for nearly three weeks while my mother lay in the intensive care unit, dearly tempted to join her husband in the Great Beyond. That was a scene repeated a number of times in the years ahead, including a long hospital stay following a heart valve replacement.

In December of 2000, my wife had emergency surgery for abdominal adhesions caused by her previous surgery for her cancer. The operation took place on the first anniversary of my dad's death (a major date in the Jewish mourning process), with our daughter in another hospital being treated again for her leukemia. I remember shuttling back and forth between hospitals, between daughter and wife, still grieving for my father, torn in more ways than imaginable.

Unfortunately, following the surgery, my wife's incision became infected, and she spent a month more in the hospital, then three months laid-up at home, while she healed from the inside out and I cleaned and dressed her foot-long wound on a daily basis. But ever so slowly she did recover.

For a while life seemed to return to almost normal as our daughter continued her chemo for the next year and then went into remission. When my mother-in-law died in July 2001, at the fairly decent old age of ninety-two, we began to hope that our lives were again on a more expected course for the first time in over two years. However, just two months later, our daughter's cancer returned, and we realized that this was not to be. (Cynically, I "thanked" God for having allowed our daughter to go into remission so that we could focus on my mother-in-law's dying because only God could have known that we could not have handled both crises simultaneously.)

In the spring of 2002, after more chemo had failed to bring our daughter's leukemia under control, she underwent a successful stem cell transplant. For the next two years we celebrated and hoped, rejoiced when she became pregnant with her second child, and held our breath as the heralded two-year point approached. But, like a marathon runner whose body gives out within sight of the finish line, her leukemia hit her again just days before the anxiously anticipated anniversary in the spring of 2004. More chemo followed, which her fetus shared, and then ultimately she endured another stem cell transplant after her baby was born prematurely. But by the summer of 2005 it was clear to even the most hope-deluded of us that there was nothing anyone could do to prevent her body's demise. We brought Amy to our house for her last few weeks so that her boys could have a refuge in their own home and Amy could have care, rest, and tranquility in ours. She died and was buried on Labor Day weekend, 2005.

Our family was devastated. My wife lost her eldest daughter, her soulmate; my two too-young grandsons lost their mother; my daughters lost an older sister; my son-in-law lost his wife and mother of his children; and I lost a stepdaughter with whom, thanks to her children, I was finally able to build a good relationship. It was just as if a huge wave and knocked us all over so that we each couldn't differentiate up from down, where the sky was or where to ground our feet. Over and over we tumbled, banging into each other as we struggled for emotional balance. But slowly, over years, our shrunken family gradually found its foothold again; we mended our souls as best we could, each one in his or her own way; and trudged on.

When my own mother finally died in July 2007 at the age of eighty-nine from a combination of mini-strokes and esophageal cancer, we believed—and life seemed to bear it out—that the cloud that had hung over our lives had at long last moved on to darken the lives of some other unfortunate souls.

Then, suddenly, three years later, in March 2010, my wife received a surprise diagnosis of metastasized ovarian cancer starting in her spleen and given less than a year to live. She followed the usual surgery and chemo routine, but the treatment wasn't working, and she suffered so much under chemotherapy that life lost its value. After three rounds of chemo, she left cancer treatment for hospice care and spent the last months of her life feeling better than she had for months' prior. But all things must come to an end, and that included her life and our time together. She died on twenty-four October 2010; she was only sixty-eight.

From her first intuition that the cancer had returned until her final breath, we had nine months. Just like a pregnancy. But where a pregnancy builds new life; cancer destroys it, slowly, inexorably. And even though we knew what was in store, in the end, when death came, it still was a terrible shock. In retrospect, it was as if yet one more huge wave, a tsunami, had come along and swept her and our future together away with one terrible inundation. My hopes and dreams littered the shore like a jumbled mass of flotsam, and nothing would ever be the same again.

Sometime after Merrily's death, it occurred to me that her two bouts with ovarian cancer provided both the opening and closing parentheses for this chapter of my life—and for this book. But my spiritual journey had begun many years before and is continuing even as I write these words. It began in earnest with my "awakening in the woods" and, while what I learned about the Jewish tradition of "arguing with God" resonated with my late adolescent conflicts with my parents (my father in particular) and other authority figures, it took these tragedies to gradually move my spiritual work from the domain of my head to the realm of my heart. While these waves of misfortune washed over us, I was constantly revising this manuscript, sharing it with friends and reading what other people had written on its subjects. It has been a work-in-progress for some eighteen years.

Initially, I was consumed with anger: anger at the God of my ancestors; anger at the vapid explanations people offered for suffering; anger with the traditional prayers that praised God continually without even a mention or a nod to all the suffering in this world; anger even at the clergy who mouthed these prayers and the people who joined in reciting them. But over time—and with a lot of work on my part—I became ever more centered once again (or maybe for the first time). This book reflects my transition from anger to acceptance to peace. And even though my reflections on the meaning of these events will always be an on-going process, I present my thinking on these subjects to you now, a summary, if you will, as I trudge on with my life and my spiritual journey.[1]

1. I think it is vitally important that we share our spiritual journeys with others, just as we routinely do bits of our life stories, because there is wisdom—and sometimes folly—in our travels and travails; information and ideas that may help others along their own paths of spiritual development. Part of the Bible's enduring appeal, I think, is that it offers stories of people in whose lives God apparently played a major role and in which, unlike real life, we are told exactly how God participated in each story.

Chapter 5

Trying to Make Sense of Suffering

The Random Terror in Life

DURING THE TIME THAT my late wife worked at Seattle's Woodland Park Zoo, I saw more than my share of films about life on the African savannah. One set of images stands out in my mind from these sorts of films: a herd of zebra suddenly erupting in terrified flight as lions charge through the herd to single one beast out for slaughter. Then, once the deed is done, the herd returns to its normal munching. The carnivore is an instrument of random terror in the daily life of the herd.

I associate this image with cars speeding along a highway. Off they go, always exceeding the speed limit, until a hidden state patrol car pounces on the unsuspecting pack. One car is singled out and halted; the rest slow down, take a look, shake their heads, and drive more slowly for a couple of minutes. Then they're off again until the next time. The speed trap is an instrument of random terror for travelers on the highway.

Human life is not much different. We go to work and live our lives, but always with a lurking awareness and a silent dread of disease and death. Then someone we know is brought down by some malady, and we offer our condolences and support, we shake our heads, utter private thanks that it wasn't us, and return to living life as normal until the next time. Disease and death—and the occasional natural catastrophe—are instruments of random terror in our daily lives.

Now the beast does not ask why the big cat chases it as prey, and we all know why a state trooper pulls over a speeding motorist, but try as we might, we can never fathom the random terror of disease and death.

For generations, humanity has tried to make sense out of suffering; each religion has offered a variety of explanations to comfort those in need. We crave a sense of order as a protection against a world of random chaos, where terror can run amok. Traditionally, God has offered that protection and I think it is human nature, nurtured in us from infancy, to want God to be—and to conceive of God as being—some sort of cosmic Super Parent, watching over us, protecting us, punishing wrong-doers, and rewarding the doers of good. So, what happens when evil befalls us?

God Is the Source of All / Not Letting the Creator Off the Hook

The so-called Abrahamic faiths[1] teach that God is actively involved in history: intervening in human affairs, selecting individuals through whom to reveal His will, testing, punishing, and rewarding individuals and whole nations based on their adherence to divinely revealed moral laws and as part of some divine plan. This traditional belief, according to which God oversees and/or controls everything that happens both to humanity as a whole and to us as individuals, is called divine providence, and it is key to these faiths.

As I wrestled with the issues of providence, suffering and evil, it has been helpful for me to differentiate between two kinds of evil. Human or moral evil is obviously the sort of suffering that we perpetrate on one another; natural evil is those natural phenomena that result in human suffering. If one believes in the traditional monotheistic Abrahamic god-concept, then God, as creator, is

---

1. Faiths based on the Bible: Rabbinic Judaism, Christianity, Islam, Baha'i, Latter Day Saints. The list goes on.

responsible for both kinds, although clearly less for the human evil because it is also believed that we humans exercise free will.

Many apologists for God's apparent inactivity and apathy in the face of human evil take refuge in the concept of free will, choosing to blame human beings completely for this kind of suffering and so let the Creator off the hook. But the rabbis of old, in their close reading of the Bible, nailed God's culpability even for human evil. In a *midrash* (rabbinic story) elaborating on Ca'in's murder of Hevel (Abel), God admits responsibility both for creating human beings with a flaw and for being an apathetic by-stander. Responding to God's question, "Where is your brother Hevel?" Ca'in retorts:

> You are He who is the guardian of all creatures and You ask of him from me? . . . I have killed him. But You created the evil inclination (*yetzer ha'ra*) in me. You are the guardian of everything, yet You allowed me to kill him. You are the one who killed him . . . for if You had accepted my sacrifice as You did his, I would not have grown jealous.[2]

God, in this *midrash*, acknowledges that Ca'in is right because the proof-text is read not just as a plea: "His blood cries out to Me (*ely*)" but also as an accusation: "His blood cries out against Me (*aly*)," because God had clearly violated one of His own commandments: "Do not stand upon the blood of your fellow."[3] According to this *midrash*, with regards to human evil, God is at least partially responsible, just as surely as is the perpetrator of the wrong.

But if God is partially responsible for human evil, which is also the result of the exercise of our free will, then God as Creator must be even more responsible for natural evil, for which there are no mediating factors. As with human evil, natural evil comes in seemingly endless variety: from events on a grand scale—earthquakes, hurricanes, tsunamis and the like—to any number of debilitating diseases, perhaps even to death itself. Every illness is a design flaw in the blueprint of Creation.

---

2. *Tanhuma*, Bereisheet/Genesis 9. See more on the evil inclination in Laytner, *Arguing with God*, 58-63 and the sources cited there.

3. *Vayikra/Leviticus* 19:16.

Mark Twain, that honest curmudgeon of a theologian, once wrote:

> Man starts in as a child and lives on diseases till the end, as a regular diet. He has mumps, measles, whooping cough, croup, tonsillitis, diphtheria, scarlet fever, almost as a matter of course. Afterward, as he goes along, his life continues to be threatened at every turn: by colds, coughs, asthma, bronchitis, itch, cholera, cancer, consumption, yellow fever, bilious fever, typhus fever, hay fever, ague, chilblains, piles, inflammation of the entrails, indigestion, toothache, earache, deafness, dumbness, blindness, influenza, chicken pox, cowpox, smallpox, liver complaint, constipation, bloody flux, warts, pimples, boils, carbuncles, abscesses, bunions, corns, tumors, fistulas, pneumonia, softening of the brain, melancholia and fifteen other kinds of insanity; dysentery, jaundice, diseases of the heart, the bones, the skin, the scalp, the spleen the kidneys, the nerves, the brain, the blood; scrofula, paralysis, leprosy, neuralgia, palsy, fits, headache, thirteen kinds of rheumatism, forty-six of gout, and a formidable supply of gross and unprintable disorders of one sort or another. Also—but why continue the list?[4]

The human condition itself is reason enough for people to be angry with God the Creator. All you need do is visit a hospital to see there more problems inherent in the human body than you could ever imagine. True, there is healing there, and that is good, but without the design flaws of the human body, what need would there be for healing?

There is a *midrash* that states that since all of God's deeds are perfect, one should not question why it is that we don't have eyes in the backs of our heads or think of other ways that God's Creation might be improved upon. I however think that we ought to imagine how things might have been—and eyes in the back of the head would be only a beginning! (And don't even get me started on the planned obsolescence of the aging human body.) This is not the best of all possible worlds unless one lacks imagination.

4. Twain, "Damned Human Race," in *Letters from the Earth*, 182.

Following Mark Twain's lead, one could make a huge list of all that is wrong with Creation and how it could stand improvement. Getting the Contractor to review the list of design flaws and to make repairs is quite another matter! But I'm willing to cut God some slack here: If God created as perfect a world as possible from the imperfect materials at hand, then He may be excused at least partially for some of Creation's problems. If, on the other hand, God created everything *ex nihilo* (out of nothing), then God has a major lawsuit on His hands for some serious design and structural flaws. Both with regards to moral evil and natural evil, God, as the Creator of all, is culpable.

This problem is further complicated by our inclination (or need) to see God's hand only in what we perceive as being good outcomes. For example, some years ago, a resident at one of Multifaith Works' homes for people living with AIDS had a very positive response to his "drug cocktail" treatment. He was ecstatic about his new T-cell levels and went about the house shouting: "It's a miracle! Praise Jesus!" In truth, this fellow's renewed health was a miracle—but I had to speak privately to him to shush him because his "miracle" upset everyone else in the house who had not been similarly "blessed." Put another way, if God was responsible for this one individual's temporary improvement, was God similarly responsible for his housemates' continued poor health? Does your mind recoil from the possibility that "God" is the source of both?

Every time I watch survivors of some catastrophe being interviewed on television, or read about them in the newspaper, I cringe, waiting to hear "Thank God I was spared," or "the Lord was watching out for me." But, although some survivors of a plane crash may attribute their survival to God's will—and many of us might have the same reaction were we in their shoes—most of us would probably shun the corollary that it must therefore also have been God's will that everyone else perish. The late Rev. Rod Romney, of Seattle First Baptist Church, told a story about how he and a carload of his fellow Baptist ministers narrowly averted a head-on collision, only because the on-coming car missed them and smashed into the car behind them. After a few minutes of shocked silence and blessed relief, one of his colleagues exclaimed "God was certainly with us there!" Romney recalls that this remark was followed by a moment of silence, before someone realized the incongruity of that statement and replied, "Yeah, but He sure let the people in that other car have it." One shrinks from this conclusion, yet many people are willing to assert that since the Creator operates with a plan, we must accept whatever happens as God's will, even perceived evils—although usually with the hoped-for caveat that they are not to happen to us. For the Rev. Romney, this was the beginning of his understanding "that often our talk about God's involvement in our lives is expressed in some rather stupid and incongruous images."[5] This bears remembering as we look at some traditional rationalizations for the problem of suffering.

A Plethora of Platitudes

Suffering presents a conundrum to most people. In most religious traditions, including those of Asian origin, there is the belief that all that happens is part of a universal plan, whether that structure is karma or divine providence. According to these beliefs, everything is explainable precisely because it occurs as part of a universal order. Therefore, when bad things happen to good people, comfort and meaning ultimately may be obtained through acceptance of one's fate, knowing that God has ordained it for our own good or that it is the working out of our particular destinies. "Submission" is the term used in Islam, and it applies equally to other faiths as well.

However, if we truly believed this, why seek medical treatment, a human intervention, when God or karma has ordained that you be ill or healthy? Why even pray for healing if God has willed you otherwise? Obviously, most of us choose not to follow this line of thinking to its logical conclusion.

We may accept the principle that everything happens according to some providential plan, but we can't accept that bad things will happen to us for no apparent reason. Why? Because, down

5. Romney, "The Changing Faces of God," sermon delivered March 13, 2005. Kate Bowler, in her wonderful book *Everything Happens for a Reason* skewers the well-intentioned, but ill-advised words of comfort people often use, particularly in Appendix I.

deep, we can't accept suffering without a good rationale (or rationalization). Consequently, particularly in the past, theologians and philosophers spent much effort to explain two sets of apparently contradictory beliefs, the first of which fits into the second: First, human beings have free will; but God is omniscient. Second, there is one God, who is omnipotent and perfectly good; but evil happens. Theologians call the attempt to vindicate or reconcile divine providence with the existence of evil "theodicy."

Put another way, we probably all can agree that "shit happens" in life. It is an experiential given, a reality. We know it when we smell it—and we know it when we are living through it. Many rationalizations (theodicies) have been written in a futile effort to sanitize this problem but, unfortunately, to assert that "bad things" are actually "good things" is like pretending that shit isn't shit. One *can* tell the difference. To pretend otherwise would be like taking leave of one's senses! Nonetheless, the efforts persist.

Over the centuries, each faith has developed a number of solutions to this dilemma, so that today (switching to a more appetizing metaphor) a sufferer has a veritable smorgasbord of rationalizations from which to choose. When I went to sample this feast, I measured each offering by how it tasted, specifically whether it masked the bitter taste in my mouth left by the Holocaust. For me, as a Jew, the Holocaust remains the zenith of human cruelty to other humans and the nadir of divine activity in the face of immense human suffering. The Holocaust poses a challenge to the validity of any of these theodicies because it applies our concepts of God and prayer, and suffering and providence, to the most extreme of life situations. This is what I call "the Holocaust litmus test": *Whatever your key theological concepts are, they must not only apply to your own life, the challenge is that they also make sense of Auschwitz.*[6] Personal tragedy can also produce its own version of this test.[7]

---

6. This is my version of my teacher (and first employer) Yitz Greenberg's "working principle," a kind of moral plumb line by which post-Holocaust theological claims should be measured: that no statement, theological or otherwise, should be made about the Holocaust that would not be credible in the presence of burning children. In "Cloud of Smoke, Pillar of Fire," 1974.

7. See Agler, *Tragedy Test*.

Here is a taste of some major explanations for suffering, primarily from the Abrahamic faith traditions, along with the reasons why I object to them—and may the scholars of religion forgive me for generalizing:

1. The most ancient but still current of Biblical answers views suffering as punishment for sins committed. Suffering is seen as a loving discipline—like corporal punishment—meant to redirect the sinner to follow God's ways. It is also expiatory, meaning that the actual suffering makes amends for the sins committed—as in "Jesus died for our sins" or the sacrificial cult in ancient Israel. According to this view, one must accept such suffering as divinely ordained punishment and then analyze one's behavior for sin and make the necessary changes. In the Bible, this view was applied both collectively and individually.[8] This explanation is still found in the traditional Jewish prayer book and echoed in popular Jewish-Christian-Islamic theology down through the ages.

I reject this explanation of suffering. It blames the victim. After World War II and the Holocaust, with sixty million killed and millions more scarred for life, this response to suffering is simply obscene. First, because it casts doubt on the character of the Judge and can lead to accusations that God is an abusive deity.[9] Second, because no sin is great enough to warrant the alleged punishment. And third, because it presumes to know the mind of God in this matter. This last objection warrants more attention.

Too often, this rationalization is invoked by religious leaders who claim to know God's will. Usually, their understanding of events reinforces their own belief system. One time I heard a sermon by an Orthodox rabbi about some Israeli soldiers. They were

8. On punishments and rewards for adhering to the Covenant, see for example *Mishlei/Proverbs* 3:33; 10:3; 11:8, 19; 12:21; 13:21; the blessings and curses in *Vayikra/Leviticus* 26 and *Dvarim/Deuteronomy* 28; the running commentary in the books of *Yehoshua/Joshua, Shoftim/Judges* and *Malachim/Kings*; and the warnings in most of the prophetic books. For suffering as discipline, see *Mishlei/Proverbs* 3:11-12. By the time of the Babylonian Exile, prophets and other writings were postulating only individual responsibility—see, for example, *Yehezkiel/Ezekiel* 18:1-4; *Yermiyahu/Jeremiah* 31:29-30 and *Eicha/Lamentations* 5:7.

9. For more on God as an abuser, see Blumenthal, *Facing the Abusing God.*

on tank patrol and the time came for morning prayers. One soldier insisted that they stop so that he could go outside, don his *tefillin* (phylacteries) and say his prayers. While he was praying, the others remained in the tank, smoking and talking. Suddenly, seemingly out of nowhere, a shell hit the tank, incinerating all those inside. The rabbi's message: Only the religiously observant Jew was spared from death because he was observing one of God's commandments. The others perished because they weren't.

People like this may also invoke God's "creation" or "use" of HIV as a means of condemning those afflicted with the disease because, in their minds, these people are sinners already: gay men, IV drug users, promiscuous people, prostitutes. Would they go so far as to deny these "sinners" medical or pastoral care since it would go against God's presumed will? I sometimes wonder.

This sort of thinking transcends religions and ideologies. After the 9/11 attacks on the World Trade Center and the Pentagon, Osama bin Laden proclaimed that the terrorists had succeeded because America was evil, and God was aligned with those who sought to fight this evil empire. Similarly, albeit from a very different religious orientation, the late Rev. Jerry Falwell, with the Rev. Pat Robertson voicing agreement, blamed civil liberties groups, feminists, gays and lesbians, "abortionists" and pagans for provoking God's anger, thereby causing God to "lift the curtain and allow the enemies of America to give us probably what we all deserve," namely the terrorist attacks on the World Trade Center and the Pentagon. By remaining theologically consistent, these clergymen made God responsible for the deaths of over 3,000 innocent souls.

There also were people who tried to rationalize the terrifying randomness of the 2004 Southeast Asian tsunami by injecting the deity into the event. Some stated that it happened because the victims hadn't accepted Jesus; others pronounced that it happened because the dead weren't good enough Muslims; still others pontificated that it was bad karma or choice of wrong livelihood. But I don't believe that "God" was in the big wave. What happened was a purely mechanistic occurrence of nature. For those who died, it was their tragic misfortune to be in the wrong place at the wrong time, and for those who survived, they were damned lucky.

Looking for God's hand in history or current events or even natural disasters is a time-honored tradition. Curiously, for most of those who believe in a God who uses natural phenomena or human activity as punitive instruments, such divinely ordained evils never seem to afflict them directly but almost miraculously only someone else. It's always easier to judge from afar.

There are grave dangers involved in this kind of causal thinking even if it does provide theological certainty. It is a theodicy with extremely troubling consequences. It is also both wrong and unjust if God, in Avraham's words, "brings death upon the innocent as well as the guilty, so that the innocent and the guilty fare alike."[10] It is distressing to believe that God would utilize some of his putative servants to slaughter other human beings. It is inconceivable that God would save some worthy souls from a disaster while allowing other equally worthy souls to perish or that God would strike some people with terminal diseases for no apparent reason and not others. It is equally monstrous that God would afflict some of the relatively righteous yet pass over (or seemingly even reward) those who are truly wicked. So, this theodicy is in fact very harmful to God's image and reputation. It is also harmful to people. *One can do serious harm to other human* beings *in presuming to know the mind of God and then telling them why they suffer.* Once someone claims to know God's will, it can lead to all kinds of violence, from religious terrorism to the bombing of abortion clinics to the shunning of people living with AIDS.

2. Suffering can also be seen as a test or trial of individual faith, such as Avraham or Iyov (Job) was subjected to. If one can endure it without losing faith and maintain one's trust in God, one will emerge spiritually more refined (not to mention being rewarded appropriately). Imagery from the Jewish tradition includes comparing the tested soul to smelted metal, which becomes purer through fire; a tree, which grows healthier through pruning; a clay pot that gets knocked to test its mettle; or a fire that, once poked, burns with renewed energy.

10. *Bereisheet/Genesis* 18:23–25.

27

Since God only tests those presumably worthy, it should be considered an honor to be chosen for "testing"—and God "never gives one more than one can handle." Furthermore, since God only tests the righteous, one ought to accept these afflictions with loving acceptance. In the Jewish tradition, this sort of suffering is called "sufferings of love." A corollary to this perspective affirms that the righteous suffer in this world in order to inherit the World to Come. If you believe in an afterlife, then indeed this reward can counterbalance suffering. However, after the Holocaust, this theodicy also is simply obscene because both the test and the character of the Examiner pale in comparison to the numbers of dead and the suffering both they and the survivors endured. And as to the reward at the End of Time—who knows?

3. Some people assert the inexplicability of suffering in combination with an attitude of submission. Individuals are encouraged to place their trust in God's goodness and in God's plan for each of us, even if it includes suffering. Whatever happens, whether good or bad, is God's will and God alone knows the reason. This is what Iyov (Job) was taught. A person simply ought to submit to God's inscrutable will and realize that whatever happens is for the best because it is divinely ordained. Having an attitude of "Don't ask" is appropriate because questioning demonstrates a lack of trust or faith in God's plan. (It's also appropriate since, in real life, "don't ask" inevitably invites a "won't tell" on God's part.)

In a way I admire those who truly believe that God is in the details; that God is intimately involved in the life experiences of each and every human being. It makes for a safer world, a more child-like world, with a protective parent hovering nearby. I admire their trust and envy their faith but shake my head at their apparent naïveté and denial of obvious experience. Nonetheless, many people find comfort in this explanation, and I must say that there *is* something very comforting about surrendering control of your life to God. It can sustain inner peace even in the face of great suffering. It keeps one's world safe, secure, and predictable even when life's experiences may well suggest otherwise. Perhaps there *is* a divine plan in which both personal and national suffering makes sense. Perhaps good people suffer in this world for sins committed and *are* rewarded in the Hereafter whereas the wicked may prosper now but will pay later. Perhaps there *is* "a divine integrity beyond our knowing" but, after the Holocaust, this response to suffering also is very offensive because what kind of God and divine plan can involve the deaths of 6 million Jews, not to mention tens of millions of other people? And that was just one genocide and one war. For that matter, what kind of God and divine plan can allow for the untimely death of even one individual?

4. Hindus and Buddhists also promote acceptance of suffering but offer a different providential plan. In the Hindu-Buddhist traditions, life's experiences—suffering and pleasure, joy and sadness—are ultimately illusory. Part of life's illusory nature is the result of our living through a series of reincarnations, and what happens in one life is partially the result of actions in previous lives. This is the process of *karmaphala*. A person's spiritual task is to attempt to comprehend the reality that exists behind the illusion by aiming for enlightenment, the transcendence of all passions and attachments. Following the various Hindu ways toward enlightenment or the Buddha's Noble Eightfold Path can speed this liberation process. How a person responds to suffering—how s/he experiences it—can affect one's long-term *karma* and therefore can help on one's way to liberation from the bonds of this illusory world.

When something bad happens to someone in these faith traditions, for example, the death of a child, it would be seen as accumulated bad *karma* from a previous life, and one should accept "the judgment" of this *karma*. But if a child dies, whose *karma* is affected? The child is most directly affected, so s/he must really have been bad in a previous life; but the parents suffer too, although not with their lives, so each must have been somewhat bad. Or perhaps *karma* works its way on both simultaneously? It would be hard to know. But *karma* as reward or punishment gives a rather profound reality to suffering that contradicts its purported illusoriness. As popularly practiced, the suffering that *karma* produces can be doubly real. Not only does the individual actually suffer but s/he may also suffer socially as well because, when bad things do happen in this life, it follows that one *must* have done wrong in a previous life, so sometimes suffering people are rejected or shunned by others for being past-life sinners. That's a problem.

5. One traditional Christian option holds that although God is omnipotent, God/Jesus chooses not to use that power in a broken unredeemed world but instead is present with us in the ordeals we suffer, even to the point of suffering with us. When we suffer, we share something with Jesus, because in human form he suffered as we do. Suffering makes human beings the wounded hands and feet of Jesus. It is certainly comforting, in a way, to realize one is not alone in one's suffering, but one has to ask: "So what? What is the tangible benefit of God suffering along with us? Where is justice? And why did God intervene actively in the past but not now?"

6. Then there are a number of theories that limit the power of God. All of these have attractive features, but all are problematic too.

Some Christian denominations embrace the existence of "Satan" as an opposing power to God. Good things come from God; bad things come from the Devil, a semi-deity. This perspective is shared by dualistic religions such as Zoroastrianism and various polytheistic religions. According to this view, human life becomes the battleground between two or more cosmic forces, and one prays to the Good God(s) for support and strength against the Bad. As a monotheist, I reject this duality of power—which is my theological bias—although sometimes is very tempting to see human evil as being demonically inspired.

According to Jewish mysticism, Creation couldn't contain the emanations of divine light that God used in the beginning and its vessels shattered, resulting in an imperfect world with a variety of evils. Our job is to act as God's partners by gathering the shards of divine light through our deeds, ultimately assisting God in restoring perfection to the world (*tikkun olam*). I love this mythic story, but I have to ask: Was Creation a mistake or a merely a miscalculation on God's part? Six days apparently can make for sloppy work!

A deist solution asserts that God is like a watchmaker who, after making the world, withdrew from the field of action to let "the machine" run on its own. God's general providence is operational in nature, but it doesn't extend to the personal level. There may be an order apparent in nature, even in how earthquakes and hurricanes operate, but the random chaos that results from catastrophic natural phenomena can be awfully hard on people and other living creatures. Thus, to some kind of general global providence, I say "Maybe; probably even yes"; but to personal providence, I say: "Show me the evidence. How does it work?" It really isn't too much to ask. Besides, I'd like to know what God has been doing since finishing the work of Creation and setting things in motion.

Some philosophers suggest that God cannot be omnipotent because then we would have no power. Rather, God is relatively omnipotent, meaning He has limited powers, and so is neither responsible for what happens nor capable of intervening. It is totally in our hands, with God only "urging" us on to do good.[11] Can this God save us from harm? Is this a God to worship? (Which is not to dismiss this perspective, only to point out its contradiction of traditional expectations of God.)

7. Lastly, a "new age" or "new thought" perspective would suggest that we are what we think. If we want wealth or health; focus on these; but if we think sick, we get sick and if we think suffering, we suffer. There is a certain truth to this because we do shape—and thus to a certain degree do control—our inner realities, but the power of positive thinking does have its limits. Death camp inmates might have been able to free their minds, but they couldn't think themselves free of their physical situations.

Theologians and philosophers keep on coming up with new rationalizations to torment the sufferer and tickle God's funny bone.[12] Of these, one critic noted that their books are "far removed from the actual pain and suffering that takes place in our world, dealing with evil as an "idea" rather than an experienced reality that rips apart people's lives."[13] All too often it seems to me that theologians

11. See Jonas, "Concept of God After Auschwitz," in Friedlander, ed., *Out of the Whirlwind*, 465-476. For an example of a process theology theodicy, see Griffin, *God, Power, and Evil*. For more on God's limited powers, see Oord, *God Can't*.

12. For some summaries of contemporary theodicies, see Griffin, *God, Power, and Evil* and Whitney, *What Are They Saying About God and Evil?*

13. Ehrman, *God's Problem*, 18.

are more concerned about reconciling their theodicies with their preconceived theologies or dogmatic convictions than in looking for a soul-satisfying way of dealing with the problem of evil.

The Holocaust, for me, has created an irreversible rift between the religious past, with its rationalizations for suffering, and the present with its questions. I do not believe that those who perished at the hands of the Nazis deserved the suffering they experienced. I do not believe their individual or collective suffering was some kind of divine testing of their mettle or a purging of sin. I do not believe that God chose to save this one or that one, while choosing or permitting others to die. I do not believe that a good God would allow the deaths of millions of people as part of some inscrutable divine plan. And I don't want to speculate about the nature of God or the origins of Creation. I would rather suffer the agony of unknowing than choose to rely on any of these gnarled answers. I want to see an end to the rationalizations, an end to theodicy.

Toward a Different Understanding of Suffering

As long as we cling to the traditional ways of looking at the issue of God and suffering, our world will remain awash with bad rationalizations. A Scottish Christian theologian, John Swinton of the University of Aberdeen, has called for a paradigm shift in how we deal with the problems of evil and suffering away from trying to explain them to presenting ways they can be resisted and transformed. He calls this "pastoral" or "practical" theodicy, a theodicy of action that focuses on practices people can learn and embody to resist evil, transform suffering and be faithful to the ideals of their faith.[14] I value his perspective and endorse his idea because of its pragmatic focus on the human being.

To try making sense of the suffering I had observed in history and experienced in my life, I found four key principles or ideas helpful. The first was to re-embrace radical monotheism, in which

14. Swinton, *Raging with Compassion*. Harold Kushner makes a similar point from a Jewish perspective in *Why Bad Things Happen to Good People*, 132–148.

everything has its source in God; the second was to affirm that there is no apparent causality between the evils that befall us and God. Third, that we must provide our own meaning to our suffering; and fourth, that we ought to cultivate a sense of inner balance at all times.

Radical Monotheism

In the Tanakh (a.k.a. the Christian Old Testament), God is the source of everything, even those things that, in our estimation, are called evil. To cite but one example of many,[15] the prophet called Ye-shayahu (Isaiah) has God declare: "I am YHVH[16] and there is none else. I form light and create darkness, I make peace (well-being) and *create evil*. I, YHVH, do all these things."[17] This is the core of radical monotheism; radical because it stands in contradiction to the popular belief that only good things come from God.

Following Yeshayahu (Isaiah)'s lead, the ancient rabbis sought to promote an attitude towards suffering that unequivocally held God responsible for all things, ordering that "A person is obligated to utter a blessing for the bad just as one utters a blessing for the good."[18] As a radical monotheist, I accept this premise and embrace

15. *Eicha/Lamentations* 3:38 and *Iyov/Job* 2:10 assert that God is the source of both good and evil. In *Shmuel One/First Samuel* 16: 14-23 God sends an evil spirit to torment Sha'ul/Saul and *Ahmos* 3:6 affirms rhetorically that God is the one who sends evil on a city.

16. YHVH is the ineffable name of the Jewish God, often rendered into English by scholars as "Yahweh" but spoken in Hebrew as "Adonai" meaning "Lord."

17. *Yeshiyahu/Isaiah* 45: 6-7. Centuries later, the rabbis incorporated this line into the daily liturgy, but with a significant change. Although they still considered God the author of all, they felt it necessary to downplay, if only for liturgical purposes, the fact that perceived evil also comes from God, so they changed the line to read: "Praised are You, LORD (YHVH) our God, ruler of the universe, who forms light and creates darkness, who makes peace and *creates all (things)*."

18. Or as one rabbi has God say in a *midrash*: "Do not behave towards Me as the heathens behave towards their gods . . . [Rather] If I bring happiness upon you give thanks, and when I bring sufferings give thanks also." See also *Babylonian Talmud*, Berachot 19a, 33b, 54a, 60b; Megillah 25a; Pesachim 50a;

the conundrum that God is the author of all. But what does it really mean to affirm that God is responsible for both the good and the bad? What are the implications in our lives?

People who can suspend their critical thinking and accept that everything happens according to some beneficent divine plan may have an easier time accepting that everything comes from God but most people, including me, only want to see God in the good and the beautiful. Although the rabbis decreed that we should thank God for the bad that happens to us as well as the good, I find this almost impossible to do when bad things happen. How contrary this is to human nature—or at least to *this* human's nature! I have no problem thanking God for all the good in my life; but the troubles and woes too? That is still a hard spiritual stretch for me—even if I accept that God is the source of all.

It is always easy to see the wonder of creation in a sunset or in a forest grove, in a newborn baby or when making love; it is almost trite to thank God when smelling a beautiful flower or seeing a spectacular vista. But it is quite another matter to appreciate the beauty in things when surrounded by a swarm of mosquitoes or to thank God for germs and bacteria that are the cause of suffering to many. Once, while working with people with AIDS, I was driving in my car and listening to an NPR "Fresh Air" radio interview by Terri Gross with Dr. David Baltimore, then head of the National Institutes of Health's AIDS Vaccine Advisory Council. I remember it to this day because what he said struck me deeply. Dr. Baltimore talked about the HIV virus in terms that can only be described as reverential: how amazing it was in structure and how ingeniously it worked. Here was a person dedicated to eradicating this horrible virus yet, in a weird way, at the same time he was in awe of this minute particle of creation; he could marvel at its intricate natural design even as he sought to destroy it. This is radical monotheism. It means embracing the totality of existence as One.

When I look at the world, I see that Creation has its apparent flaws as well as its observable beauties, but overall, I think that Creation itself, though morally neutral, is generally speaking, overall

---

and the *Tziduk HaDin* prayer of the Jewish funeral service, and *Arguing with God*, 103-115.

"good." From our limited and self-interested perspective, we perceive some events as good and others not, but—as God pointed out to Iyov (Job)—we know diddlysquat about how the system operates as a whole. It is important to remember that none of us is the center of the universe, even if our self-centered, narcissistic being tries to claim otherwise.

Whether an event is good or bad is a matter of perceptions—it is based on how we process or interpret life experiences at any given moment. The same sun whose light I consider a blessing today may simultaneously be someone else's cursed drought-maker. Whose view is correct? Neither person's; it is only a matter of perspective—and even that view may change as we change.

Thus, the ultimate challenge is to be able to appreciate the mystery and wonder—the awe-fullness—of an earthquake or a disease, even as one is struck with horror and sadness. It is hard to reconcile these two aspects of natural evil—the wonder with the terror—yet it is essential to do so in order to acknowledge unity of all things under God's Oneness. That is radical monotheism.

No Causality

Equally important to me is the rejection of a belief that is almost bred in the bone: I force myself *to choose not to make* any causal connection between what happens in life and "God," who is the source of all. What this means in practical terms is that I believe there is a high degree of randomness to life in terms of who is killed in an earthquake or who survives a car crash, or who gets AIDS or cancer and who survives. Even when it comes to human evils, in the end they often affect innocent lives just as randomly as natural evils do. They all have their source in God, yet none is caused by God.

Of course, events that might be perceived as miracles do happen. One person might inexplicably be cured of cancer; another might survive a massacre. Both likely would call their salvation miraculous and they would be right to do so in the sense that it is inexplicable and incredibly lucky. But I draw the line when it comes to asserting that God was responsible. I strive to marvel at the totality of creation, even at the terrible awesome power of so-called natural evils and the awfulness of human evils, but I never ascribe their occurrence to God's will. What happens seems mostly a matter of chance—dumb luck—and the choices we make as a result. Put more simply: Life is a crapshoot; what matters only is that you try to go with the roll and mitigate any negative consequences.

Making Meaning

Because life appears to be a process of random chaos, with no rhyme or reason to it, I am challenged to provide my own meaning to its events. I believe a life experience acquires meaning solely by what we choose to impose on the experience, and on what we learn from that experience for better or for worse.

In *Man's Search for Meaning*, Victor Frankl observed that Jews incarcerated in Nazi concentration camps stood a better chance of surviving (assuming they weren't carted off to the gas chambers) if they were able to imbue their lives with meaning. The same holds true for people with chronic and terminal medical conditions, and people dealing with grief issues.

Many a person with AIDS told me that only getting that terrible diagnosis made them turn their lives around and cease their self-destructive behaviors. Their impending deaths often gave their lives meaning and purpose—usually to educate others about preventing the spread of the disease or encouraging people to volunteer to help. This search for meaning is a way to transcend the tragedy of our most terrible personal experiences. In meaning lies purpose, and in purpose there is hope, and hope feeds life.

Why do some people suffer more than others? I am not referring here about physical pain, although that too is experienced differently by each of us, but rather about emotional struggle and spiritual suffering. When something "bad" happens, it presents a challenge to one's personal integrity, i.e., one's sense of wholeness, and to the meaning one finds in, or provides to, that experience.

There have been numerous Jewish, Christian and Muslim martyrs who died gruesome deaths yet never suffered spiritually.

They did not, because they knew they were more than their bodies, that their lives and deaths were part of something larger, and they had faith or trust that there was an order to their world—a belief in a divine plan and in a World-to-Come that could sustain them even when in unimaginable physical pain. Their sense of connectedness with God never wavered and that gave them hope; it allowed them to maintain their wholeness.

Now consider the case of Iyov (Job). Iyov was a righteous man who suffered spiritually because he could not reconcile his experience with the commonplace perception that suffering only came as a result of sin. After being afflicted with tragedy and physical suffering, he also endured spiritual suffering, induced in large measure after his so-called friends began to "comfort" him. This led him to question God's justice as it applied to his personal situation. Iyov suffered because his sense of meaning in life was turned upside down. Based on his understanding of how the world was supposed to operate, he could not accept what had happened because it made no sense, and he did not have the inner strength to cope with adversity *and* the torment of his friends' insensitivity. As a result, he suffered spiritual alienation, a sense of isolation from God's presence.

Fortunately for Iyov—and how unlike so many of us!—he received an answer directly from God. From his revelatory experience, Iyov learned that a) what had happened to him was an insignificant part of the greater mystery of Creation, b) that it had nothing to do with justice or sin, c) that God cared enough to put in a personal appearance, and d) that God approved of his protests. It was the divine appearance that restored Job's sense of connectedness with God even though the lesson learned—that there is no justice manifest in suffering and that what occurs in life is part of something so vast that one can never comprehend it—was at best cold comfort. Creation is too vast, too complex, for us to comprehend in its totality. A little humility was called for in Iyov's case, just as it is in ours. But at the same time, as God later notes, it was Iyov who in his anger had spoken appropriately of God, not his friends, who spouted the popular rationalizations of their era.

For us, the meaning of suffering is not found by asking "why?" but by asking "to what end?" or "what is the invitation in this experience?" A pregnant woman endures the pain of childbirth because she knows (or hopes) that something good will emerge, that a baby will be born. But other sorts of pain, physical and emotional and spiritual, are not so clearly productive. It remains for us to shape the offspring of that experience.

Do you "find" meaning in an experience of suffering or do you "make" meaning for such an experience? The difference is profound. The former implies that the meaning exists in the experience, perhaps even that God has something specific in mind in whatever happens to each and every one of us. The latter, on the other hand, suggests that experience itself is a *tabula rasa*, a blank slate, on which we can inscribe, or create, whatever meaning we wish, for good or bad, for life or death. Whatever happens to us in life is what it is; whatever we make of it is what it will mean. That is our only option.

Suffering is a fearsome teacher. Some people lose faith in the course of suffering; others gain it. Some people are destroyed by the experience; others manage to heal. People who suffer physically may or may not suffer spiritually. I have seen both. Working with people with AIDS, I saw some transform their pain into creative, positive energy; but I also saw others turn their suffering in on themselves and wither from within. Our personal contexts may not be so extreme, but we all make this same choice, for better or for worse, at many different points in our lives, because living is a series of choices, of certain potentialities or possibilities pursued and others denied. Every experience is either a stepping-stone or a millstone, depending on how we respond to it, how we reflect on it, and how we use it.

Cultivating Inner Balance

According to the concept of the stages of grief, either Kübler-Ross' or some other model, "acceptance" is one of the final steps in the emotional healing process. Like the cycle of grief, suffering has its stages in which anger is as appropriate as acceptance. The goal ultimately is "acceptance," which means making spiritual peace with one's changed situation. Most people go through a series of emotional/spiritual peaks and valleys that mark their back-and-forth struggle to deal with grief or adversity.

However, in many of our faith traditions, fatalism is often confused with faith and acquiescence with acceptance. For many people, displaying a lack of emotion during times of emotional or spiritual turmoil, and thereby denying anger, depression and the like, may demonstrate fatalism not faith; not acceptance of what has happened but acquiescence to an apparent abusive power beyond their control; not serenity but the suppression of honest grief and anger. The result is that many people consider passivity and the repression of "negative" feelings to be the proper responses to suffering of a truly pious person. We may aspire to respond like martyrs when "bad" things happen to us and then berate ourselves (or others) for reacting like Iyov, outraged at God for what has befallen us.

I would never suggest that it is goodly, or godly, to suffer in silence or that we should squelch our emotions in times of trouble. We human beings have every right to be upset if our expectations in life get thwarted by the random attacks of disease or death. In most cycles of grief, there is also a place for anger and protest; why not for people of faith too? For Jews, this concept might not be as foreign as it may be to other peoples because we have good role models of protest down through the ages. I believe in the value of argument and protest because they can help reorient ourselves in a period of crisis and turmoil. To lament or protest one's fate or that of a loved one is the opposite of resignation; it is an assertion of self and power exactly at a time when the events are conspiring to rob you of both. Protest and anger can be good tools if they help us transition to the stage of accepting that what is, is.

Suffering can be a lonely state of being. It can alienate you from your body; it can alienate you from other people; it can alienate you from your sense of connection with God. Isolation in all these ways only makes suffering worse. The challenge for those of us who accompany loved ones on these dolorous journeys is to keep our lips shut and our hearts open, so that the person at the center of the storm can voice the concerns of his or her soul, regardless of how they sound to our ears.

The key to providing suffering with positive meaning is acceptance. When life is taken as it is, when you release yourself from your expectations for the future and from your illusion of control, then you can begin the birthing process of transforming what was into what is, and let what will be, be. But it is not easy to do.

Personally, I try to cultivate internal balance regardless of what happens in my life. Equanimity would be an appropriate word if one understands this to be an inner state rather than outward composure because anger, tears, laughter, and every other emotion have been my steps along the way towards an acceptance of what has happened and a return to the world of the living.

A Christian friend (I wish I could remember who it was) once told me that, in her tradition, she was taught "to look for the grace in everything," meaning that God gives us something to learn from every experience, even bad ones. It seems to me that there is a certain psychological value and spiritual wisdom in "looking for the grace in everything" or "praising God for the good and the bad" because by doing this kind of reflection one may come to an eventual acceptance of whatever has happened.

I believe that nothing that happens comes directly from God, yet I see no contradiction between my Christian friend's affirmation and my own. To my mind, these apparently contradictory ideas are two sides of the same coin. To believe that nothing comes directly from God is almost the same as believing that everything comes from God. Both attitudes can lead to a state of acceptance. In my own time of crisis, I found I could almost repeat the words of Iyov, "YHVH (The LORD) has given, and YHVH has taken away; blessed be the name YHVH" except that I uttered: "The process of life gives, and the process of life takes away; blessed is the process of life."

I find my comfort and my meaning in a God who may hopefully "accompany" me in some mysterious way throughout my life's experiences but who apparently directs nothing; a God who may "listen" when I pray but who apparently does nothing in response. In my God's non-action, I may find strength and solace, but I find my comfort and my meaning in relying on myself and on my fellow human beings to do on earth that which many have expected God to do for them. If God's presence is anywhere, it is in our individual and collective responses to life's challenges. With this evolving sense of God and this understanding of suffering, I am personally better able to deal with the random terrors of life.

The Hebrew word for "whole" (*shalem*) and the word for "peace" (*shalom*) share the same root (sh-l-m), as does the Hebrew expression "*refuah shleimah*," meaning "get better" but literally "a whole (or complete) healing." Like the modern understanding of the cycle of grief, the Jewish model for recovery is a circle, with a return to wholeness and peace being the desired ends. Healing, wisdom and ultimately peace come through striving to transcend the buffeting of life, by seeking the spiritual learning moment in everything, and in remaining connected with the divine, however conceived. Whether one understands what happens in life to be part of God's plan or not, that is for each of us to decide for ourselves. But, regardless of how you achieve it, acquiring a sense of acceptance of your fortune can make suffering endurable and perceiving a sense of unity with a divine presence can suffuse suffering with hope for a better future.

Chapter 6

The Awe-fullness of God
Strikes Me Down

WHENEVER I TAUGHT OR lectured about "arguing with God" I always introduced my audiences to the protests and prayers of previous generations, but I would never "pray" them directly to God, nor would I lead my listeners in prayers of protest. I was too self-conscious to try, and perhaps I lacked belief in its efficacy, but I also knew I was I was a coward at heart when it came to confronting God and I feared to try praying this way in public. My reticence made my "arm too short to box with God." And so, instead, I kept on repeating the same message over and over again: "It's kosher to be angry at God and to use prayer as a form of protest. Look—here's a who's who of who has argued with God in the past: Avraham, Moshe, Yermiyahu (Jeremiah), Iyov. Think about all we've suffered: Babylonians, Romans, Crusader massacres, European expulsions, Cossack massacres, Russian pogroms, the Holocaust. Come on! We should all shout those words from Paddy Chayefsky's film *Network*: 'We're mad as hell and we're not going to take it anymore!' Now that's a modern Jewish prayer!" Then we'd all laugh rather nervously, relieved that I had not actually led them in such an angry prayer. No harm done. It was all just an intellectual exercise. . .

It was also a personal spiritual dead end. "Arguing with God" had been my spiritual practice for decades, but I had taken it as far as I could. Without a Biblical-type divine response, how long can one go on protesting? I knew I needed a new direction, but I had a dilemma: I had built a mighty scholarly tower around me to bolster my perspective from attack and my ego was heavily invested in my subject. But the problem with building a tower from the inside is that, once completed, one is enclosed, and I ended up being trapped in a spiritual cell of my own making. It was becoming clear that I needed to break out—or be broken out.

With every class I taught, every service I led, every sermon I gave, I brought myself closer and closer to some ill-defined edge. Then, one Rosh Hashanah, I skirted a little too close to that edge, leaned over and confronted that which is nameless, awe-full, and fearsome. I was struck down in a heap. (Or so it appeared to me.)

One of the Torah portions read on Rosh Hashanah is the story of the binding, or near-sacrifice, of Yitzhak (Isaac), by his father Avraham, at God's command, and of God's last-minute intervention to prevent that sacrifice from occurring. Traditionally, the story is viewed as a test of Avraham's faithfulness and his complete trust in God and/or as a test of Yitzhak's willingness to be a sacrifice, a martyr. That particular year, I wanted to preach on whether we can know what God really wants of us. I wanted people specifically to ask themselves how Avraham knew that what he heard as God's command to sacrifice his son actually was God's command and not some dark deviancy of his own devising. To dramatize this idea, I planned to read God's words in the Torah portion in a stage whisper rather than chanted aloud as is customary.

I was in fine form that day, confident and self-assured. But by the third line of the Torah reading, I knew I was in trouble. Perhaps it was the fact that I hadn't eaten that morning; perhaps it was due to my lack of voice training that made me hyperventilate as I stage-whispered God's words; perhaps I was ambushed by the dramatic emotional effect the recitation had on me—to this day I do not know for sure—but I choked on the words, grew hot and then light-headed, and finally broke away from the lectern to collapse in a faint.

Pandemonium broke out in the congregation. Now, had this been an evangelical Christian church, everyone might have been on their feet shouting, "Praise Jesus!" at this outbreak of the holy spirit, but since this was a Reform Jewish congregation, people cried out,

"Oy gevalt! Is there a doctor in the house?" Surprisingly, there was only one. I came to with a hundred faces anxiously peering down at me. I took something to drink and a candy, finished services and later let my wife take me for a check-up. The doctor said I had a tendency towards hypoglycemia and told me that I had to eat regularly.

That explained everything. . .

But it didn't really, because I alone knew what I had been feeling as I had grown dizzy. As I whispered God's words, I thought of my own little daughter—or was it me as a son?—and what it really would mean to be commanded to kill one's own child and then actually to seek to do it. I felt a dread overcome me, my blood congealed in my belly, I shrank back in horror, attempted to flee—and fainted dead away. For the next ten days I was literally without energy, a nervous wreck. I managed to lead Yom Kippur services only by holding, white-knuckled, onto the lectern.

When I look back on this awe-full event, I realize that all explanations as to why I fainted are valid and probable. My doctor and my therapist and my friend the actor all had their own rationales, but I have mine. I choose to remember the event primarily as a spiritual experience, and not a very pleasant one at that. I had been touched by the dread of the divine and reminded of the limits of my power. I was jolted to move on in my spiritual journey. I came to recognize the temptations of the ego in the pulpit, to understand my power and its limits, and to realize the awesome responsibility that I, as a rabbi, hold with regards to other people. I learned to take seriously what I offered, but what I sometimes had presented too flippantly. In short, I learned humility.

Like Yaakov after wrestling with God's messenger, I still "limp" because of that encounter. For a long time, I was silent. I had lost all confidence in my voice. I turned down speaking engagements, refused to lead worship services. It was only after I took a job helping people living with AIDS that I began to heal my inner wounds. But it was years before I had the fortitude to speak again in public, although never without some degree of anxiety that I might be "struck down" again.

Chapter 7

My Problem with Petitionary Prayer

The Holocaust versus the Exodus

WHILE OUR FAMILY WAS in the midst of its dark night, some of us turned to uttering prayers for divine intervention. But none of our pleas for healing or mercy were answered—not at least in the way that we wanted. This, for me, ended whatever residual attachment I had for the type of prayer that asks God to do certain things. Experience had taught me otherwise. I finally came to accept that this kind of prayer, called petitionary prayer, doesn't pass my "Holocaust litmus test" because our mundane requests for divine intervention made no sense in the light of how the prayers—the life-in-the-face-of-death appeals—uttered by people in situations like Auschwitz, were ignored.

Blame my problem on the Bible. Simply stated, the stories of God's miraculous interventions into history as recorded in the Bible stand in stark contradiction to the darker realities of human life ever since, raising the question about why God apparently answered some people in need at one time but not others in equally dire need later on. It's an ages-old conundrum and it runs through many faiths, not just Judaism.

In a Jewish framework, the tension is created between two poles, one which may be called "the Exodus" and its opposite, which is typified as "the Holocaust." At issue is God's consistency. "The Exodus" stands for "expectation," as represented by those Biblical stories in which God intervenes in human life, while "the Holocaust" stands for "history," the post-Biblical historical experience, in which God doesn't. The two contradict each other. *Either* God's intervention during the Exodus from Egypt is somehow true *or* our historical experience is true, but both can't be true without something having to give way. The contradiction shows the classic dilemma of theodicy.

If both are right then that would mean that on one occasion God chose to intervene while at another time God chose not to, or that at one time God acted with compassion but at another time God chose not to. To hold that both are true leaves God open to charges of being cruel and heartless, indifferent to human suffering, and deaf to pleas for mercy. And let me say it: a capricious God, or a cruel and abusive God, is worse than none at all!

On the one hand, if the Exodus story is accurate, then we ought to question where God's saving power was during the Holocaust. Or, on the other hand, if our experience of the Holocaust is true (and we know it is), then we should question our continued adherence to the concept of a supernatural God who actively intervenes in the course of human life and history.

This, in a nutshell is my problem with prayer as it pertains to suffering: To put it crassly, can we really expect that God would pay attention to petty petitions such as for supporting one's favorite football team or finding a parking place when that same God apparently ignored the prayers of the many people who died in any one of humanity's countless genocides or in natural disasters?

Then too, each of us must wrestle with the suffering, pain, and death that make life such a challenging experience. Many people, no doubt, have feelings of anger and abandonment; many question the absence of God's saving presence or protest against God's perceived indifference to their fates. Many end up rejecting traditional doctrines about God and the role of prayer, as did Rabbi Richard

Agler, in *The Tragedy Test*, following the death of his daughter in a horrible accident.

The Exodus story symbolically has always been in tension with the suffering of the present. That tension remains because people refuse to let go of the hope for divine succor yet there is also no escaping from the reality of their experience of suffering. The result of this cognitive dissonance perhaps accounts for the large numbers of religiously unaffiliated people in America, people exploring alternative religious traditions and, paradoxically, the numbers of people turning to more "fundamentalist" forms of faith. The problem isn't confined to the Jewish people alone.[1]

A second part of my problem with traditional prayer has to do with how we Jews pray. To be a Jew—or a member of any group—is to wrestle with one's inherited traditions. I think many Jews do to themselves in prayer what the Japanese do to trees in bonsai: we prune our natural spiritual inclinations to fit the prescribed shapes of the traditional modes of prayer and the traditional concepts of God. I'm sure we're not unique in this practice. I think it is what many religions do with basic human spirituality.[2]

I have great respect for people of any faith who can invest a liturgy with the yearnings of their souls, who can still relate to a personal supernatural God; and I salute those clergy who strive to

1. See, for example, Bass, *Grounded.*

2. I think there is a great fear in some quarters about unbridled spiritual expression. There always has been. For one thing, it threatens those with the power and authority to determine what proper orthodox behavior is and what is not. It can undermine belief, lead people down strange unauthorized paths. Imagine the kinds of prayers people might have offered and the things they might have said to God, if allowed, immediately after the Holocaust. Imagine what individuals might say in the depths of suffering from illness or grief. Imagine the myriad of different ways of prayer and forms of ritual and ideas that might exist today if people's spirituality had been less restricted by religious authorities over the centuries. Far better, in their minds, to keep things under tight control so that our world and our concepts of God are not unduly disturbed. In these ways liturgies are harmful. But liturgies are also beneficial. They affirm common beliefs, shared praise, and sanctioned requests. They confirm the group identity. They assert values and sustain hope. And all that really is fine with me—after all, I *am* a rabbi, invested in preserving our people's traditions.

make the traditional prayers more relevant to contemporary congregations. For me, however, usually the ancient words just get in the way, although singing them in Hebrew makes the prayers easier to swallow, just as the song says that a spoonful of sugar helps the medicine go down, because singing engages a different part of the brain and heart. But I must ask myself: "Why go to such lengths to provide meaning to words that no longer fit our views? Why not just create something new, something that works for us today?"

A third component of my problem with prayer has to do with how prayer is expressed: On some level, I consider prayer, any sort of articulated prayer, to be like blasphemy because it limits and constrains God, either by whatever words we can fathom to use, or because of the expectations our prayers put on God. During the time when the Jewish liturgy was being created, at least some of the ancient rabbis recognized the absurdity of trying to use human language to praise a Being as mysterious and ineffable as God.

In one Talmudic story, a man improvised on the traditional prayers by adding to God's praise as follows "the great, the mighty the awesome, the glorious, the powerful, the valiant, the fearless, the strong, the sure, and the honored." Rabbi Hanina waited patiently until he finished and then said to him: "Are you all through? Why did you stop when you did? Did you finish all the praises of God? Why all these extra words? Even the three words of praise we do say, if Moshe (Moses) had not mentioned them in the Torah . . . we would not be allowed to recite even these three. Yet you say all this and keep going on and on!"[3] On the one hand, it boggles the mind to imagine trying to communicate with an essentially ineffable Presence but, on the other hand, there has hardly been a society in human history that has not assumed the ability to interact with the divine in some way. This remains a basic desire for most people.

Lastly, I have a serious problem with the limited tone of prayer. In most faith traditions, public prayer is limited to praise, petition, penitence, and thanksgiving. But how do you pray to God with all the hostile feelings that accompany the experience of suffering? In a troubled human relationship, negative feelings are communicated,

3. *Babylonian Talmud*, Berachot 33b.

more or less effectively, to the other person involved. But when the other party is "God," then the form of communication is called prayer and, in most traditions, including the normative Jewish one, prayers that give voice to negative sentiments would be considered impious or even blasphemous. Anger and protest and lamenting are not considered appropriate in tone for addressing "our Father in Heaven." So how does one pray when bad things happen to basically good people? How do you pray the intense feelings that go with that?

Prayer as Protest

Traditionally there were a number of responses that Jews have used to deal with the problem raised by unwarranted suffering. To review these: one route blames the victim and says that God punishes people with suffering for their sins. A second well-accepted path praises the victim(s) by saying that God only tests the righteous and affirms that the righteous suffer in this world in order to inherit the World-to-Come. A third well-established track rejects questioning because questioning demonstrates a lack of trust or faith in God's plan. But the response that intrigues me the most is what I call "arguing with God" because it endeavors to hold fast to both ends of the Exodus/Experience contradiction. Never mind that one party is the Creator, God Almighty, and the other, is God's creation, a creature of dust and ashes. The two are bound together by a covenant (*brit*, in Hebrew), which is basically a contract or agreement, a rather unique way of framing the divine-human relationship.

Because of the Covenant, both the Jewish people and God have the right to take the other party to task if said party is not fulfilling the terms of the Covenant. In the Bible, it is usually God speaking through the prophets taking the king and/or the people to task for idolatry or ethical lapses; but sometimes it is the prophets or the psalmists criticizing God for apathy or inactivity in the face of injustice and oppression. In the "arguing with God" stance, when bad things happened, God might simultaneously be praised for the events of the Exodus and reproached for failing to intervene in the tragedy of the day. In this way, the people's expectation to see God's ultimate justice was affirmed, but their feelings of anger and abandonment also were articulated in prayers of protest. It is a tradition that goes back all the way to Avraham, the first Jew, and continues down to our own day.

Consider the following examples:

In Tehillim (Psalms) 44, God's great acts in the past are celebrated: "We have heard with our ears, O God, our ancestors have told us what deeds you performed in their time, in the days of old." But then just a few stanzas later come harsh accusations:

> Yet You have rejected and disgraced us . . . You let them devour us like sheep; You disperse us among the nations . . . All this has come upon us, yet we have not forgotten You or been false to Your covenant . . . Rouse Yourself; why do You sleep, O Lord? . . . Why do You hide Your face, ignoring our affliction and distress? Arise and help us, redeem us, as befits Your faithfulness.

Words like these are both a protest *and* an argument, or at least one side of an argument. God's apparent inactivity is questioned—but God's power and authority are not—because the expectation is that God will respond; that God will answer their protest with action.

Jewish suffering over the centuries has made a case for a sustained argument with God, often based on the Exodus precedent. Centuries later, in rabbinic stories (*midrash*) dealing with the destruction of the Second Temple and the oppression in Roman times, the rabbis set the following prayer in the mouths of their character, a personified Israel:

> Master of the Universe! You did wonders for our ancestors, will You not do them for us? . . . What a work You performed in bringing them forth out of Egypt and dividing the sea for them! But You have not done anything like that for us! . . . You did it for them, but not for us . . . When will You work a good sign for us? . . . 'Show us Your mercy, O Lord, and grant us Your salvation.'[4]

This being *midrash*, God responds: "Indeed I shall be favorable to you also" and Psalm 85:2 is cited as proof of God's intentions in the

---

4. *Midrash Tehillim* 44:1.

future to restore Israel to its land. Anger, complaint, a plea and a word of divine comfort—it was a good message for the people to hear in those difficult, trying times.

Centuries later, during the time of the Crusader massacres in Europe, rabbi-poets wrote poem-prayers called *piyyutim*, and many of these continued this quarrel with God. In one of these prayers of protest, the author plays savagely on the words of Exodus 15:11: "Who is like You among the mighty (*elim*), Lord?" He adds one letter to the word *elim* so it becomes *elmim*, with the result that the verse now reads: "Who is like You among the dumb, Lord!"

> Who is like You among the dumb, my God? You kept silence. You were silent when they destroyed Your Temple. You remained silent when the wicked trod Your children underfoot . . . We came through fire, water and flame. They mastered us, stoned us, and hung us on scaffolds. They rode on our heads, but we declared our love for You. We descended into Sheol while living and we were swallowed . . . You are the zealous one and avenger, where then is Your vengeance?[5]

This poem-prayer is all the more audacious because it plays most seriously on the opening line of a major prayer in the Jewish liturgy that celebrates God's intervention at the Sea of Reeds.

Another poem, written during the terrible Khmelnitsky pogroms in seventeenth century Ukraine, demanded: "When will the day of the final miracles come? Your sons and Your daughters are given into the hands of an alien nation and Your eyes see! Show us Your miracles as during our Exodus from Egypt!"[6]

And even now, in our post-Holocaust era, the Jewish quarrel with God continues, although today it is our poets and authors, not rabbis, who continue the tradition. Consider excerpts from this poem by Friedrich Torberg, an Austrian Jew who made it to America in 1940, regarding the Passover seder:

5. The full text of Yitzhak bar Shalom's poem "There is None Like You Among the Dumb," in Hebrew and English, with notes and commentary, can be found in Petuchowski, *Theology and Poetry*, 56-62.

6. Gavriel ben Yehoshua Strassberg of Raisha (17th C), "How Can I Lift My Face?" quoted in Dubnow, *History of the Jews*, 4:48.

Lord, I am not one of the just.
Don't ask me, Lord, for I could not answer.
I do not know, you see, why for your servants here
this night is so different
from all the others. Why?

The youngest child was happy once
to learn the answer at the table feast:
Because we were slaves in Egypt,
in bondage to wicked Pharaoh
thousands of years ago . . .

And because, O Lord, you led us forth
with an outstretched arm
and delivered us from oppression and grief
and treacheries numbering a thousand,
we sit, reclining, and break into crumpling pieces
our fathers' bread of affliction . . .

And so we give thee thanks, O Lord,
for saving us from harm,
as we gather believing
today, and here, and in every land,
and "next year in Jerusalem."

The youngest child who heard all this
has long since lost his faith.
The answer of old no longer holds,
for "next year" never came, O Lord,
and the night weighs down heavy and dark.

We still have not wandered across the sand.
we still have not seen the Promised Land,
we still have not eaten the bread of the free,
we still have not done with the bitter herbs.

For time and again in our weary wanderings
Pharaoh has set upon our trail,
behind us he comes with his bloody henchmen—
the carts, O Lord, do you hear their clatter—
O Lord, where have you led us to!

You sent us on without a star,
we stand at the shore and stare on high,
O Lord, the flood has not returned,
O Lord, the night is not yet past,
"Why is this night so different from. . ."[7]

Prayers of protest such as these, while perhaps sounding blasphemous to our ears, were all backhanded ways of affirming the belief in God's ultimate justice and mercy, just as surely as the normative prayers did. Once the protest was lodged, it was assumed that, at some point in the future, God would make things right. The point is that *if* God had not saved Israel from Egyptian bondage, *then* there would be no expectation that God would save Israel again. But, since it is traditionally believed that God *did* save Israel in Egypt—that God *does* watch over humanity and that God *does* intervene in history—then, when experience contradicted expectation, prayers of protest were one response that the people and their spiritual leaders chose to utilize to voice their anguish.

The experience of suffering is always personal and sometimes collective. In either case, it is traumatic, and the pain must be articulated if any healing is to occur. Today, if we truly want to be honest, not only to God and the Biblical accounts, but also to our own experience, then we should try expressing our anger with God when we gather to pray in response to tragedies and/or when we gather to mourn and grieve over loved ones. If we believe that God is the Creator and Preserver of all, then doing this might be efficacious, if not to rouse God to action, then at least for us in our pain.

My "quarrel with God" has gone on for many decades, at least since the 1970s.[8] It is encouraging to see that, over the years, the

7. Torberg, "Seder, 1944," in Schwartz and Rudolf, *Voices within the Ark*, 980–81. Torberg's "blasphemy" is mild compared to other post-Holocaust poets. Consider this short prayer by Perets Markish, part of a much longer poem called The Mound, written response to Ukrainian pogroms of 1919–20, "I yearn to merge with you in prayer/And yet my heart, my lips are moved/Only to blasphemies and curses" in Howe, Wisse, and Shmeruk, ed. *The Penguin Book of Modern Yiddish Verse*, 358.

8. William Morrow notes that Claus Westermann and Walter Brueggemann began their pioneering work in this field as it pertained to Biblical

"arguing with God" approach has gained currency in segments of both the Jewish and Christian worlds and also been applied in a broad variety of situations. David Blumenthal utilizes both the accounts of survivors of child sexual abuse and of the Holocaust to make the case for prayers of protest against an often-abusive God, Dov Weiss has explored the rabbinic roots of confronting God in a wonderfully detailed scholarly book, and Shmuel Boteach attempts to use the tradition of "arguing with God" to reconcile suffering with traditional Judaism and its view of God. In Christian circles, Kathleen Billman and Daniel Migliore, and John Swinton, explore the pastoral and spiritual dimensions of the lament if it were to be adopted as part of Christian usage, while William Morrow believes ours is an age that will see a revival of prayers of protest in Jewish worship and for the first time in Christian prayer too, and Peter Admirand writes that the ubiquity of human suffering takes the need for protest global.[9] For people still wrestling with a traditional, supernatural God, these developments are all for the better because, by advocating for the inclusion of prayers of protest, they make a relationship with that kind of God more honest and more complete.

Although I am no longer in my "arguing with God" phase of spirituality, I still believe that people should be encouraged to use prayer to express their feelings of anger, betrayal, abandonment, and injustice; that they shouldn't sit on their feelings and pretend that nothing bad has happened and that all is well between them and God. I still believe that there is a need, and that there should be a place, for individual and collective prayers of protest and anger because prayer should reflect the reality of experience and God—whatever God is—should be big enough and tough enough to be able to handle honest communication from the likes of us. It is both theologically and psychologically sound.

---

studies in the 1970s, precisely when I also began my research into this subject as a young rabbinical student. See Morrow, *Protest Against God*, 3, n. 8-10.

9. Blumenthal, *Facing the Abusing God*; Weiss, *Pious Irreverence*; Boteach, *Wrestling with the Divine*; Billman and Migliore, *Rachel's Cry*; Swinton, *Raging with Compassion*; Morrow, *Protest Against God*; Admirand, *Amidst Mass Atrocity and the Rubble of Theology*.

The Future of Prayer

I think that the need to "pray" is innate and can help as we deal with suffering. Humankind has always prayed and will always pray. Perhaps, as Nicholas Wade has suggested, we are born with a faith instinct.[10] Certainly I have seen it firsthand in my children and grandchildren as they try to puzzle out life, death, and things beyond. It is as if they each discover "god" independently and then seek confirmation from the adults in their lives (who at that point probably will provide religious education/indoctrination rather than engaging in the spiritual discussion that is called for). I don't think that the need for faith, which I prefer to call spirituality, will ever die; religions may evolve or vanish, but people will continually reach for something transcendent beyond their mortal existence, seeking a sense of connection or comfort or something else yet again that will help inform their finite lives with meaning and support. That is the purpose of prayer: it's about having a relationship with the divine, however understood. This means that in its purest form prayer is about connecting with the divine, i.e., having a spiritual experience and therefore everything else—all the words of praise, petition, penitence, and even protest—is secondary.

So, prayer, in some form, is here to stay. The ways humanity prays are diverse and have changed radically over time. Two thousand years ago, animal sacrifices were the dominant form of worship around the world. Eventually sacrifices were replaced in most cultures by rituals of prayer and song. During this same period, our various conceptions of God also changed, although not necessarily with any awareness of our having done so. Today, when most of us look at the idea of offering animal sacrifices to God, we are likely to exclaim: "What were these people thinking? Did they really believe God wanted *that*?!" Similarly, I think that, in the future, our way of relating to God will be as dramatically different from worship as practiced today as today's practice of prayer is from when sacrifices were the dominant mode of worship. Someday people may look at the prayers we've been using for the past several millennia—all those words of praise, self-abasement or dogmatic assertion—and

10. Wade, *The Faith Instinct*.

bemusedly ask: "What were these people thinking? Did they really believe God wanted *that*?!"

After my year as an interim congregational rabbi, where one of my major tasks was to serve as the communal prayer leader, I feel more certain than ever that prayer as we do it currently belongs to an era of the past. This is not to say that the ancient prayers do not speak to people—and even to me—still. These prayers ask of God what people seek for themselves: health, sustenance, understanding, forgiveness, contentment, peace. They also affirm the values that people cherish: trustworthiness, gratitude, slowness to anger, forgiveness, compassion, justice, love, and love of peace. They just project these desires outwardly, as petitions, to God in Heaven.

But here's the rub: what to replace traditional prayer with? Prayer is unlike any other activity in that it can imbue diverse individual human beings with a sense of community and simultaneously connect that community with the divine and with their ancestors in a way that touches both head and heart. What other activity can aim to do all that?

I think that prayer should embrace expressions of gratitude and allow for feelings of anger; it should involve silence and meditation, and song and praise; and it should include the opportunity for personal reflection and transformation. Prayers for healing and comfort could be offered, not in the sense of alerting God to the need for intervention, but to make the community aware of its members' needs for support. Music should play a key role because music taps into a different part of our brains; it can reach into our souls and touch us in a different way than merely reading words aloud does. And ritual will be there because ritual seems to be as basic to our nature as "the faith instinct." We humans love rituals; we use them everywhere to mark all kinds of occasions, both religious and secular; and events frivolous or serious; so ritual—ancient or modern, traditional or creative—will continue in some form as well.

I see three essential components to prayer in the future: contemplation, personal transformation, and gratitude.

Contemplation

The Talmud tells us that what God requires of us in prayer is the heart.[11] Regardless of the forms of prayer we utilize, "the heart"—intentionality (*kavana*)—is what must be cultivated, and it is a highly personal endeavor.

The contemplative traditions all offer an old/new way of connecting with the divine that is different than our normative way of praying. A number of rabbis, priests and pastors are developing contemporary forms of contemplative prayer.[12] Contemplation helps us cultivate our intentionality in order to connect with the divine and to achieve inner balance. The challenge as I see it is how to build a sense of community and collective purpose from an activity (or a form of prayer) that is essentially a personal experience. The challenge doesn't obviate the value of contemplation, it just complicates its use. (This problem I happily leave to others to work out.)

Personal Transformation

In Hebrew, the word for "to pray" is "hitpalel," a reflexive verb meaning in its root "to judge oneself." To me, this is indicative that, at its core, Jewish prayer was supposed to be personal and self-transformative rather than externally focused. I find transformational or reflexive prayer rather appealing because its focus is on changing the attitude of the one who prays rather than asking God to intervene in some way. This form of prayer is self-directed: "May I find within me the wisdom to deal with this issue." Reflexive prayer makes sense to me because it aims to transform the person making it.

A former co-worker, Ed Shields, a maverick Catholic priest, used to think that prayer was "begging God to do something or give something" but, over many years, has gradually shifted his

11. *Babylonian Talmud*, Sanhedrin 106b.

12. Fr. Thomas Keating's "centering prayer" movement is a contemporary contemplative form of Christian prayer, and Rabbis Rami Shapiro, Ted Falcon, Yoel Glick, the late Alan Lew and others have tapped into the Jewish mystical tradition to revive (and adapt) Jewish meditative forms of communal worship.

perspective. This is how the now-internalized process of reflexive prayer works for him:

> More and more, I see prayer as changing me or putting me in line with God's thinking. I express my feelings honestly to God. Then I look at how I might respond to the issue that troubles me . . . Then I realize hopefully that this issue or event is an opportunity to respond with compassion and with love. My prayer then moves me and not God. This is not an easy or always successful process, but I am working at it. Often it takes some time to arrive at my being changed or moved.[13]

According to the rabbis, even God uses the reflexive form of prayer. Consider "God's own personal prayer" as imagined by the rabbis:

> May it be My will that My compassion may overcome My anger, and that it may prevail over My attributes of justice and judgment, and that I may deal with My children according to the attribute of compassion, and that I may not act towards them according to the strict line of justice.[14]

As much as it may help God, it is also a prayer I use regularly in my own life to encourage my better inclinations.

Transformational prayers enable you to focus on your needs, to center your energy and intention, to find hope, but without raising the expectation that God will respond by intervening directly. What we ask for, hope for, and expect of God when we offer petitionary prayers is what we really need from ourselves and one another: trust, compassion, justice, mercy, love, forgiveness, saving acts, peace-making and so on. Reflexive prayers can help us to focus on, celebrate, and actualize those values that we hold most dear. They allow us to focus on the power for good that resides within each of us to bring it out in its fullest possible expression in the world. Like traditional prayer, it builds hope for a better future. What matters is that whatever kind of prayer you do should help

13. Personal communication.
14. *Babylonian Talmud*, Berachot 7a.

you learn to stay centered and to be able to transcend whatever happens in life and to adapt in response to those experiences. The key is an attitudinal shift and that is what these reflexive prayers consciously seek to accomplish.

Gratitude

Thankfulness remains for me something worth praying about, regardless of how one views God. Albert Einstein once said that there are two ways of going through life: one is as though nothing is a miracle; the other is as though everything is a miracle. It all depends on attitude. I choose to look at life as a miracle and gratitude is my response—even when things seem bad. For example, my attachment to my late wife and my grief over the loss of our future together caused me much pain and suffering. But that same attachment—the love we shared and the life we built together for ourselves and our family—is also a reason for profound and abiding gratitude. I am grateful despite my sadness.

Traditionally, when we give thanks or praise to God then, ideally speaking, it means that we are consciously articulating an inner awareness of the manifold gifts we receive from the Creator of All. Rabbi Abraham Joshua Heschel called this attitude towards life one of "radical amazement." A wholly holy person would not be someone with an episodic sense of wonder; s/he would have a consciousness of a divine connection and an attitude of radical gratitude every minute of every day. (That may be what being enlightened is all about.)

However, recognizing that most human beings are unable to attain or maintain this exalted state, the rabbis of yore sought to elevate people's souls at least occasionally. They decreed, for example, that a person ought to recite at least one hundred blessings each day: for waking from sleep, for the working of our bodies, for our ability to perform God's will, for the gift of Torah and its commandments, for the food we eat and the clothes we wear, for life itself and whatever it may bring. These "gratitudes," as I call them, are examples of everyday mysticism, an opportunity to develop a deeper spiritual awareness in daily life.

While I struggle with the inadequacy of words to express feelings to and about God, I am truly aware of the gift of life and of the unique potentiality it holds, despite all my family has gone through. You cannot work with people living with AIDS, as I did; or go through too many, too-close encounters with death, as our family has, without it sharpening your appreciation of the true fragility of life, and of its unique preciousness and value. Once touched by suffering and death, you never forget, and you are never the same.

But you don't need a brush with mortality to be reminded of the miracle of life and of life's opportunities. This can be had every moment of every day. There is a Jewish prayer that traditionally is said upon arising each day: "I am grateful to You, living and enduring God, for restoring my soul to me in compassion. Great is Your faithfulness." Prayers such as this one still work for me on some level because they help me maintain "right attitude" and "right perspective," reminding me of the fact that whatever I enjoy in life begins simply and most mysteriously with the life to which I awaken each and every morning so far.

Another example: We don't talk about bodily functions in polite society. In fact, there are only two occasions when discussion of bodily functions is socially acceptable: when there is a baby present or when someone is sick. And so it was that when my late wife was recuperating from her abdominal surgery that the first words out of the surgeon's mouth to her were: "Got gas?"

"How rude!" is what I immediately thought. And I made a joke about it.

But then the surgeon explained. "Gas is good," she said. "Gas is a sign of vitality. If we don't produce gas in our intestines, we are in big trouble because it means our bowels aren't working as they should." (Descartes should have said: "I fart, therefore I am.")

Working with people living with AIDS makes one aware of the importance of nitty-gritty things like gas and bowels. We all share their concerns, although not perhaps with the same intensity, but how important these things are! If our bowel movements are too frequent, we complain; if they're too infrequent, we complain. If they don't happen at all or if they happen all the time, we die. The human body is a finely balanced mechanism. When problems occur, it is the little things that matter so, for the smooth operation of our bodies, we should be grateful regularly.

In Jewish custom, there is prayer that thanks God for making our bodies work the way they do, which is said after going to the toilet.[15] Perhaps it seems odd to you, perhaps not, to thank God for having formed our bodies with the ability to work as they do, but to pass gas, to have a bowel movement, etc., are as much miracles of creation as is viewing a mountain vista or a spectacular sunset, would that we were uninhibited enough to be willing to acknowledge them as such. Gratitude is what is called for.

Personally, I look for ways to express gratitude regardless of what I happen to encounter in life. When things were at their darkest in my life—as when, on the first anniversary of my father's still-too-sudden death, I was told that my wife had to have emergency abdominal surgery, while our daughter was lying in another hospital trying to cope with the aftereffects of chemotherapy for her leukemia—or even more, as my wife lay dying ten years later—I could still find a thing or two for which to be grateful: for love, for life itself, for time spent together. I was grateful even though I cried with stress and incredible grief. Gratefulness does not necessarily mean happiness. I find it in tears as well as in smiles. Radical gratefulness is a matter of right mindfulness—of staying in the here and now, focusing, and being aware. I however find it simply impossible to remain continually aware of the exquisitely painful/wondrous impermanence of existence and I cannot begin to appreciate Creation and life enough, let alone to express what I feel.[16]

The key thing for me is to try to maintain this sense of radical gratefulness as I go about my daily routines. When I remember to

15. "Praised are You, YHVH our God, Ruler of the universe, who has formed human beings in wisdom, and created in them many openings and vessels. It is well known before your glorious throne that if but one of these doesn't work properly, it would be impossible to exist and stand before you. Praised are you, YHVH, healer of all flesh, who does wonders."

16. David Steindl-Rast has written and taught much about radical gratefulness. See, for example, his book *Gratefulness, the Heart of Prayer.*

try, I can uncover a sense of radical wonder and a corresponding need to express radical gratefulness for just about everything, regardless of my situation—even if I don't use the traditional blessings to acknowledge it. But, in truth, despite my best efforts, I often take far too much for granted. To help me stay focused and aware, I went through a period when I took to muttering an ancient Jewish blessing, one that traditionally is used just on holidays, special occasions, and for all things new. I call it the "Jewish centering prayer" because it helps one center on the miracle of the present moment, to focus on preciousness of any given point in time, and to be grateful for its holiness: "Praised are You, YHVH our God, Ruler of All, who has given us life, kept us alive, and enabled us to reach this moment."[17]

Ancient prayers such as this one still speak to me, albeit in a non-traditional way. In general, though, as I try to cultivate an attitude of radical gratefulness, or when I offer a reflexive prayer, or when I meditate, I find that what the Psalmist said long ago[18] still works best for me: "To You, silence is praise." And so, for now, I find that my silently-articulated feelings brought to conscious mind are my best, most heartfelt prayers, and I am grateful simply for being alive and alive to life's wonders and pains.

17. To my surprise, one evening when I met my friend Rabbi Ted Falcon for our pre-COVID sushi and sake suppers, he began the evening with a toast using this blessing in exactly the same way as I do. He told me it's been his common practice for some time as well. He teaches that blessing opens us to the wonders of gratitude, and gratitude is the doorway to living in the present moment.

18. *Tehillim/Psalms* 65:2

Chapter 8

The One Time I Offered a Personal Prayer of Protest

IN 1999, SOME YEARS after my collapse, my sister-in-law, Jane, died quickly, tragically, and far too young, of a brain tumor. At the same time, my wife, Merrily, was struggling to cope with ovarian cancer. We all were emotionally devastated so, rather than conducting the funeral service myself, I asked a rabbinical colleague to do it. Instead, I decided, despite my anxiety, to offer a reflection/prayer for those of us—myself, family members and friends—who had trouble accepting what had happened, and who could not in good conscience utter the compliant, pious words required of us by the traditional Jewish funeral liturgy. It was my intention to speak honestly about things, but even more importantly, I also hoped my words would be therapeutic or pastoral, meant to begin moving us from anger toward acceptance.

I started off by quoting the troublesome lines from the Jewish funeral service:

> The Rock, His work is perfect; for all His ways are just; a God of faithfulness and without iniquity. The Rock, perfect in all His deeds: Who dares say, "What is it that You do?" to Him who rules above and below, who takes away life and gives it, who brings down to the grave and raises up. Righteous are You, Adonai, in taking away or giving life, for in Your hand are pledged all spirits. We know,

Adonai, that Your judgments are right, Your decrees just, and Your rulings pure. None should presume to question Your judgments. Praised be the True Judge.

Then I interjected:

"But we do question; we do protest! Ribbono Shel Olam, Ruler of the World, I call you to task for breaking two of your own Commandments.

"You have murdered and You have stolen. With this cancer, part of Your creation, You have murdered first Michael, and now Jane, cut them down in the prime of their lives. With it, You also threaten the life of their sister, Merrily. And, as if this were not enough, You have stolen. You have stolen precious years that ought to have belonged to Jane. You have stolen years of love and companionship from her, from her husband, from her mother, from her sister, from her children, from her beloved grandchildren, and from her many friends and colleagues. Dear God, it is intolerable what You put us through sometimes!

"And yet, what choice do we have? Whatever happens, happens. There is no way to avoid this truth of existence. Is it preferable to ascribe all things to God's will as our tradition holds, or is it better to call life a random series of events and experiences, without sense or order? That is for each of us to determine for ourselves.

"In the end, we can only accept what happens, whether we believe it comes from God or not. There is no choice but to accept. Even in this case, even with our Jane. We can only accept and continue on, dealing with our feelings of loss and grief as best we can.

"So, dear God, although we must accept what has happened, and what happens every day all around us, that does not mean that we accept it as Your will. We cannot, we will not, offer words of praise to You if indeed this was Your deed.

"But we can offer thanks for the very existence of this wonderful woman, for how Jane touched our many lives in so many different ways: as child, sister, wife, mother, in-law, grandmother, friend, colleague, and therapist. Though her life was too short by half, she lived it passionately, intensely, and we are all better for having had her as a portion of our own life experiences. Her life was indeed a blessing to us all.

"For having known her, and for having loved her, and for having been loved by her, we gather now both to honor her memory and praise Your Holy Name. Amen."

This was the only occasion on which I have been brave enough to actually "argue with God." Unlike that fateful Rosh HaShannah morning years earlier, nothing bad happened to me. I was not struck down for my *chutzpah*. My anger was my own and my heart was pure in its prayer of protest. While I spoke it, no one uttered a sound, and after the burial service many people came up to thank me for articulating what had been lurking unspoken in their hearts.

Chapter 9

A Voice from the Dead Changes My Life Direction

IN THE 1980S AND early 90s, I was working as Community Relations Director for the Jewish Federation of Greater Seattle. My job was to bring together the diverse organizations and congregations in the Jewish community—Orthodox, Conservative, Reform and the non-religious; Democrats and Republicans; hawkish Zionists and dovish Zionists; and more besides—and to work with them to seek consensus positions on issues both domestic and international. Practically speaking, this was a thankless task because it meant that I was either being criticized by the left wing for being too conservative or attacked by the right wing for being too liberal. (No one ever asked me what I personally thought.) After ten years of this stereophonic *kvetching*, I had developed an awful headache and knew I needed to move on to a new position. But until I found it, I was locked in my career, just as I found myself spiritually blocked by arguing with God as well. That's when a voice from the dead gave me the encouragement to forge a new direction for my life:

I was riding in my car, returning home from having taught yet one more class on the Jewish tradition of arguing with God. My new cassette of Bob Marley and the Wailers was on the tape deck. I was listening intently, enjoying the music and the message. And then I heard it, Bob Marley chanting from beyond the grave: "One love, one

heart, let's get together and feel all right. . .If Anson prays to the Lord,
then it will be all right."

I nearly drove off the road! Talk about reefer madness—could he
really be addressing me? What was he telling me about my stubborn
refusal to pray to the God for whom I only had anger? I was shaking as
I rewound the tape and played it again. Ah, there was the problem—it
was his Jamaican accent: "One love, one heart, let's get together and
feel all right. . .(G)ive (d)ance-an(d) praise to the Lord, then I will be
all right." "Give dance and praise"—not "if Anson prays." I chuckled
with relief and laughed at my own foolishness.

But as I listened to the song again and again—and, although
I now knew Bob Marley wasn't addressing me specifically (thank
God)—I realized that he was talking to me, soothing me, telling me it
was time, time to let go of some of my anger, to open my soul to love,
my heart to joy, and my being to compassion. Perhaps, by doing these
things, there would even come a day when I would let myself be able
to pray again. He told me: "Don't worry about a thing, 'cause every
little thing gonna be all right . . . this is my message to you."

Soon after, I took a new job for the better when I was hired
as the executive director of the Multifaith Works, a non-profit or-
ganization that provided supportive housing and spiritual care to
people living with and dying from AIDS. It was 1993 and AIDS was
a major crisis in America; then still an illness that provoked fear
and loathing in many people's minds.

I was done with consensus statements and talk without action, so helping people who really needed support and doing so on
an interfaith basis greatly appealed to me. Despite my misgivings
about doing pastoral work, and knowing next to nothing about gay
culture, I began working with people who faced disease and death
on a daily basis. It was a plunge into the deep end of human suffering, and it changed my life completely.

At Multifaith Works, I commenced an apprenticeship in the
practice of lovingkindness under the tutelage of some of the most
wonderful people I have ever known. Whether co-worker or client
or volunteer, all conspired, as it were, to help me climb out of the
spiritual hole I had dug for myself by focusing solely and for too
long on arguing with God.

Working with people with AIDS forced me to confront the issue of personal suffering head-on. I observed that many individuals dealing with a terminal illness react to suffering no differently than does the collective consciousness of an entire people. Both wrestle with the issue of God's presence in the face of suffering: "Where is God when suffering happens?" "Does God know what is happening?" "Is God responsible for my suffering?" "Did I do something to deserve this?" "Who or what is God?"

As we struggled together through grief, remorse, anger and bewilderment, I began to look at God in new ways, to view pastoral counseling and prayer with new respect, to see how much our various faith traditions have in common, and to regard hands-on service as one of the best ways to live one's faith. It is an adage in the AIDS community that, in helping others, a person in fact gets more than s/he gives, and I have found this to be so for me as well. I learned so much about life, about other people, and about myself. I know I became a more compassionate and less judgmental human being as a result.

Chapter 10

What I Learned from the Chinese Jews

As I WRESTLED WITH the meaning of suffering and God's role in it, struggling to make sense of it all—a process that took years—unbeknownst to me at the time, I was being influenced by my parallel interest in the Chinese Jews of Kaifeng. Influenced—or perhaps guided? Was it serendipity or something more? Who knows? Regardless, how I came to study the Chinese Jews and their impact on me is a story in itself.

My China Connections

How did I come to be so interested in the Kaifeng Jewish community? And why did I major in Chinese Studies if I intended to enter the rabbinate? I often get asked these questions. The truth is that, although I don't believe in either divine plans or in destiny (are these the same?), nonetheless even I am surprised by the number of coincidences that have shaped my experience with the Jews of Kaifeng, China.

As a young man in his first week at York University in Toronto, I more or less fell into Chinese Studies because of a woman, an electrical power failure, and a forced choice. As is common at many universities, York requires its entering students to take a core curriculum that included a science, a language, a humanities and so on. I duly registered for a science course and found myself sitting with several hundred other students in a modern, windowless lecture hall listening to a professor introduce his course. Suddenly the lights went out and, while we sat in total darkness, the professor kept on talking as if we could take notes. "This sucks," is what I remember thinking to myself. Later, as I told a woman friend from high school about this incident, she said that I should consider doing my language requirement first and save the science course for another semester. She told me that she was taking modern Chinese with a newly arrived teacher from mainland China and the class only had six students in it. I was doubly intrigued—first by my woman friend, and second by the prospect of meeting someone from the People's Republic, virtually a unique opportunity in 1969. I switched courses and thus entered the world of Chinese Studies. Had the power not failed *and* my friend not been so enthusiastic about the course *and* had I not been required to take a language course, I would never have embarked on the path I did. Coincidence number one.

A second coincidence: I "discovered" the Chinese Jews of Kaifeng by accident while wandering the East Asian Library stacks at the University and coming upon a hefty volume in the entitled *Chinese Jews* by Bishop William Charles White, who had headed the Anglican mission in Kaifeng back at the beginning of the twentieth century. To my surprise I read that White also was from Toronto, that his book was published by the University of Toronto, and that the Royal Ontario Museum (ROM) was the recipient of many of the artifacts he acquired while in China, including items from the now-destroyed Kaifeng synagogue. For years I had visited the ROM and wandered by the Kaifeng artifacts, completely unaware of their significance until I came across White's book.

And a third: When I applied to participate on the first Canada-People's Republic of China Student Exchange Program, one of my interviewers turned out to be a young Jewish professor of Chinese Studies named René Goldman. Once he learned of my interest in the Kaifeng Jewish community, he told me that in 1957 he, then a Polish citizen, and another Sinologist, a Czech man, had toured Kaifeng and insisted on meeting some Jewish descendants despite repeated official denials of their existence. Eventually they got their wish and were permitted to meet an elderly Jewish couple to whom they introduced themselves as Jews. Theirs was the only direct contact with the Kaifeng Jews from the late 1940s until 1980, when Kaifeng opened up again to foreign visitors. I was one of the few people to know of his visit there. (When I lived in China in 1973-74, I tried unsuccessfully to travel to Kaifeng, but it was still closed to foreigners on account of the Cultural Revolution.)

Another coincidence: 1976 found me in Cincinnati, Ohio on the campus of the Hebrew Union College (HUC) beginning my second year of rabbinical school. (The first year is spent in Israel doing intensive Hebrew language study.) Once at HUC Cincinnati, I found out that its Klau Library is one of the main repositories of manuscripts from the Kaifeng Jews and the librarians allowed me to see their collection in the rare books room.

Knowing of my interest in the subject, when Michael Pollak contacted the HUC Klau librarians regarding research he was do-ing for his celebrated book *Mandarins, Jews and Missionaries*, they put me in touch with him and I shared Goldman's story with him, which he included in his book. Nine years later, Pollak was kind enough to include me in the gathering of scholars and activists in Palo Alto that led to the founding of the Sino-Judaic Institute. Though I was young, I was asked to edit its journal *Points East* from my home in Seattle, which I do to this day.

And lastly: One day I received a letter addressed to me as the editor of *Points East* from nearby Victoria, British Columbia. It was from a former professor of mine at York University, a Jewish Sinologist named Jordan Paper, now deceased, who had attempted to teach me classical Chinese. He had retired and relocated to Victoria with his wife and was reaching out to me in my capacity as editor of *Points East*. It was a surprising and happy reunion for the both of us. Years later, he asked me to write a postscript to his book *The Theology of the Chinese Jews, 1000-1850*, in which I at-tempted for the first time to apply the theology of Chinese Jews to the contemporary post-Holocaust Jewish experience, and later he and I edited a collection of scholarly essays on the Kaifeng Jews past and present.[1] Although I did not realize it until he and I worked together, I had begun a process of integrating their ideas into my own personal spiritual search as well.

How the Kaifeng Jewish Experience Helped My Spiritual Growth

We often have no idea of the extent to which Judaism has borrowed from other theologies and philosophies down through the ages. This is what Jews everywhere have always done in order to survive and grow. Because they lived in China, the Kaifeng Jews borrowed from Daoist and Confucian thought as they settled into their new cultural home. In no small part due to its small population size and isolation, the Chinese Jews assimilated almost to the point of disappearance while, further to the West, foreign ideas were assimilated into Jewish culture, but the Jewish communities flourished.[2]

Nonetheless, the incorporation of Chinese ideas into Kaifeng Jewish religious thought represents a unique synthesis. Admittedly, this Sino-Judaism has not had any influence in the history of Jewish thought as did, for example, the incorporation of Hellenistic thought into proto-rabbinic Judaism, which evolved into the Judaism that is practiced today, and which also laid some of the foundations for Christianity and Islam, but it is nonetheless significant in its own right.

The Kaifeng Jews wanted to have their faith and practices be understood in light of the dominant culture, much as Jews everywhere always have. In the Chinese situation, they were fortunate to live in a society that fostered syncretism, and which was indifferent

---

1. Laytner and Paper, *Chinese Jews of Kaifeng*.

2. Paper in *The Theology of the Chinese Jews* has drawn attention to the cultural bias of the dominant Ashkenazi Jewish community, which renders the Jewish culture of so-called "exotic" Jewish communities "inauthentic." Its attitude towards the Kaifeng community is part and parcel of this bias. Thus, while it may indeed be said that the Chinese Jews absorbed foreign ideas into their faith, the same should be said about the Jewish communities of Europe and the Middle East as well. What is fit for the Beijing duck ought to be fit for the goose and gander as well!

to doctrinal differences in a way unimaginable in the monotheistic Middle East, North Africa, or Europe. Consequently, the Kaifeng community was able to embrace basic Confucian and Daoist concepts and relatively easily blend them with their own Jewish ones. The focus of both Confucianism and Judaism on human relationships rather than theology made this synthesis particularly rich and it was able to sustain the community for many centuries.[3]

As I struggled professionally and personally with Jewish spirituality—and as I was simultaneously learning more about the Kaifeng Jews—I began to think that perhaps the Kaifeng Jewish materials, recorded for posterity by Jesuit and Protestant missionaries, might have something of value to offer the spiritually restless souls of our post-Holocaust, contemporary world. What I didn't realize at the time was that it would be spiritually worthwhile for me as well.

When talking about God, the Kaifeng texts use the term *Tian*, which is not a proper name or even a word meaning "God," like the Hebrew *El* or *Elohim*. Like its Hebrew counterpart "*Shamayim*," *Tian* is a word with a dual meaning, referring both to the actual sky and to a figurative or symbolic "Heaven." It is impersonal, even abstract. Rather than using the anthropomorphisms of the Torah, Talmud and prayer book—terms like father, king and so on—the Chinese Jewish texts assert that the divine, i.e., Heaven, is a mystery, as something truly beyond our comprehension. This is hardly an alien idea for it is precisely what some of the prophets, Jewish philosophers (Maimonides, for example), and the Jewish mystics taught as well.

The biggest difference between the Chinese Jewish "theology" and mainstream Jewish theology has to do with the concepts of revelation and God's intervention in history. In the Chinese Jewish texts, *Tian*, Heaven, can be perceived through the creative power of nature and through the Torah, both of which are called the *Dao* (or Way) of Heaven. Revelation is the attunement of the human being with the *Dao*, which is omnipresent and immanent. It is the role of

3. That the Kaifeng community almost ceased to exist is due to its small numbers and long isolation, to the integration of its members into the larger society, and to China's own long eclipse during the late Qing dynasty and the subsequent turmoil of the early Republic.

the exceptional human being to perceive it, experience it, and try to communicate it to other people.

In the Chinese Jewish view, it is through human endeavor and self-improvement that an outstanding person like Avraham or Moshe can gain enlightenment and perceive the *Dao* of Heaven. In Avraham's case, his enlightened state made him the first to "know" Heaven and therefore he is honored as the founder of the faith. In Moshe's case, his highly developed personal character led to his perceiving the mystery of Heaven and then to his composing the Scriptures and the commandments therein. But the revelation was theirs to achieve, not God's to bestow. Absent from the texts is any substantive reference to Yisrael's miraculous exodus from Egypt or its biblical years, or to God's use of history and nature as either reward or punishment.

Lastly, what emerges as most striking about the Kaifeng Jewish materials is their humanistic focus. The ordinary person has only to practice the *Dao* as expressed in the Torah, i.e., doing the *mitzvot*, or commandments—honoring Heaven with appropriate prayers and rituals, respecting one's ancestors, and living ethically—in order to put oneself in harmony simultaneously with the *Dao* of the natural world and the *Dao* of Heaven. For the Chinese Jews, as for Jews everywhere, the *mitzvot*, the commandments, provide for Jewish continuity. They constitute "Jewish civilization" and, wherever Jews wandered, there too went the *mitzvot*. The Kaifeng Jews were traditionalists in their observance, but they embellished their practice with Chinese values. Their adoption and adaptation of the Chinese value *ziran* (self-awareness) stressed the importance of personal spiritual development and the need for self-evaluation/self-cultivation as an integral part of observing the *mitzvot*. One is engaged in *ziran* not just for one's own sake, but because one's personal ethical behavior both shows respect for one's ancestors and provides a model for future generations to emulate.

This sense of connection with the past and future was probably heightened for the Kaifeng Jews by their adoption of Chinese cultural norms of *xiao* (filial piety) and "ancestor reverence." Although much more intense than normative Jewish practice, *xiao* has its counterparts in commandments such as honoring one's parents and respecting elders, and in mourning customs such as observing the anniversaries of one's parents' deaths. Ancestor reverence gave them a unique sense of being contemporary links in the chain of a proud and ancient civilization. It was a way of honoring and connecting with the past and emphasizing the responsibility of the present generation to prepare the way for the future.

What I appreciated from my study of the Kaifeng Jews' theology was their emphasis on human behavior combined with ritual practice, and on the ability of individuals to perceive an immanent Presence in the world. Their thinking provided me with an alternative to a system based on a supernatural God's intervening in history and waiting for God to intervene in history once again. Theirs was a faith firmly planted on earth and grounded in the proper doing of daily deeds. Their practice was meant to enable them to feel a sense of unity with past and future generations, with the totality of the natural world and with Heaven itself.

What came to matter most to me from my study of this community was its emphasis on inwardness. It was what I wanted for myself. While I knew a little about the contemplative tradition in Jewish mysticism and Hasidism, that didn't resonate with me the way the Kaifeng Judeo-Daoist approach did. Probably it had to do with the complex theologizing and cosmology of the former and the simplicity of the latter, which stressed attunement and mystery. Regardless, from their Sino-Judaic synthesis I felt a historical validation that meditation and seeking union with the divine were legitimate Jewish activities. Their teachings came to inform my desire to seek balance and harmony and inner peace in life; to accept both good and evil as part of life; and to aspire for a connection between my mind/heart, soul/*neshama*/*chi*, and God/*Tian*/YHVH/the *Dao*.

Chapter 11

Letting Go of "God" to Find God

HAVING REJECTED THE VARIOUS rationalizations for God's inactivity in the face of human suffering and consequently admitting the futility of praying to God to intervene, I gradually came to the realization that I also needed to let go of the traditional view of God, an awareness fostered by my studies of the Kaifeng Jews.

Naked Spirituality

In the Abrahamic traditions, when we consider God, we usually start from the heavens and look down, the point of departure being God's purported self-revelation in our holy books. Instead, we should start with ourselves and pursue the subject of knowing God further from the ground up.[1]

Imagine a naked person. In terms of physical characteristics, we all look basically the same—we are, after all, one species. Now put clothes on that naked body. The wearing of clothes is something we all do yet at the same time we also use clothes to distinguish us, one from the other, in terms of culture, class, generation, and gender.

---

1. My friend, Mary Jane Francis, an Episcopal priest, has told me that Anglican Christianity also does theology "from below," meaning that it starts with experience and builds from there.

Now imagine that naked person again. In terms of general spiritual characteristics, we also are basically the same. Every person, by virtue of being a human being, shares certain spiritual characteristics, just as we do physical ones. These include: the desire to have meaning in one's life, to know love and feel companionship, to have a set of morals and values, to live a life of hope, and to sense some connection with something that transcends the individual self.

I find it hard to imagine that are any people without spiritual issues when confronting suffering and death. When we confront our mortality, we might find ourselves facing spiritual needs and issues that had been long and deeply suppressed, such as completing unfinished business in one's relationships; concerns about love, reconciliation, and forgiveness; anxiety about one's deeds and misdeeds; and of course—or perhaps, questions about God and the hereafter. When a crisis hits, these issues and needs acquire an urgency they never had previously, and to face these crises without any spiritual clothing can be cold indeed!

Most people use a faith community (whether inherited or chosen) to cover and express their naked spirituality. Our various religions are the spiritual clothes we wear, yet at the same time we also use them to distinguish us, one from the other. Just as material clothing comes in a variety of styles, so too do religions offer various designs for belief, life cycle rituals, forms of worship, and types of community. And, over time, each faith grows more and more specific about what clothes (i.e., the beliefs and rituals) its adherents may or may not wear.

At one point or another in their lives, many people will look at the spiritual clothes they are wearing and ask themselves if they really are a good fit. Perhaps they've gotten a little too constrictive, maybe they are too juvenile in appearance, or just plain out-of-date. As people examine their spiritual outfits, they cannot help but focus on the central feature of each outfit: God. How humanity has styled God down through the ages has resulted in a variety of conflicting high-end design concepts. God is singular or plural; visible or invisible; transcendent or immanent or both; male, female, both and neither; eternal, resurrecting or reincarnating; etc., etc. Religions are hard-pressed to confine perceptions of God to just a few authorized fashion statements.

In my case, I grew up comfortably wearing Jewish spiritual clothes. Later, after my experience of the divine, some of these clothes no longer fit quite right. My "arguing with God" outfit was the last spiritual outfit that featured a traditional conception of God. The more I probed conventional rationalizations for suffering and other beliefs about the traditional God, the more I realized I had to try on a spiritual outfit that was designed around a different God-concept. I needed a different way to think about God.

God is Greater

At one stage in my life, I focused my time on pondering the meaning of the Covenant and the special relationship Jewish tradition says Jews have with God. Today the issue of being God's "chosen people" seems too parochial; it seems absurd to think this way any longer. Can God really be so concerned with the affairs of one, small people? Yes, the Jewishly-perceived God can be; and the Christianly-perceived God is equally concerned about the Church. Indeed, I wonder if there is a nation or a faith anywhere that has not considered itself "God's chosen" or "beloved," the figurative center of the world or most important country/tribe/faith of all. Individually and collectively we never seem to completely lose our child-like desire to be the center of the universe, the apple of God's eye.

Today, however, the world is smaller than it once was; we know more than ever before about one another thanks to advances in travel and communication. We now know that many faiths and peoples have considered themselves God's favorite. But, even in the best expressions of traditional religion, the universal God of the Jews is still attached to the Jews and the Land of Israel; the universal God of Christianity is bonded only to the Church; the universal God of Islam reveals His word only in Arabic—and even Zen Buddhist ceremonies, rituals and meditation are best performed Japanese style!

Our efforts at describing God are like the story of the blind men and the elephant. Six blind men were asked to determine what an elephant looked like by feeling different parts of the elephant's body. One blind man felt a leg and said the elephant was like a pillar; the one who felt the tail said the elephant was like a rope; the one who felt the trunk said the elephant was thick as a tree limb; the one who felt the ear said the elephant was broad and flat like a hand fan; the one who felt the side said the elephant was like a wall; and the one who felt the tusk said the elephant was like a pipe.

Was any of them wrong? No. But was any one of them completely right? No again.

None of them could see what an entire elephant looks like and so identified the whole by the part they had felt. In fact, however, an elephant has all the features they experienced and more.

I use this famous story to describe our relationship with God. All of our faiths agree that what we call God is ultimately an indescribable mystery to limited creatures such as ourselves. But then we then turn around and insist on defining God by our limited experiences, just like the blind men in the parable. However, God is beyond all these borders of our own perceptions. Rather, God belongs to us all, no matter how we choose to dress and address the divine.

I liken God to an infinitely faceted gemstone, one that simultaneously offers many different perspectives for observation. Each individual, each generation and every faith over time can describe only a few divine facets—but no one individual and no one faith can ever know the whole "gemstone"—that remains beyond our human capabilities. But put all the facets together and you get a much better picture of how humanity imagines God.

In the end, our theologies are identically flawed because they are all limited by our human capabilities to know. Nonetheless, they also all point to a shared truth: That humanity perceives there is something somehow greater than all of us. Each religion has a unique perspective of this "Presence" and has designed distinctive spiritual outfits—systems of belief and practice—based upon that perspective. There is unique validity to each perception of "God" and to every religious system built upon those perceptions. But our theologies are our metaphysical constructs, not eternal verities. They represent conceptions based upon perceptions of "God"; they do not represent "God" the ineffable, who exceeds all our imaginings, past, present, and future. The sum of God concepts is greater than all its parts and the total will always amount to mystery.

What is called for is a little spiritual humility on our part. Spiritual humility means realizing that whatever we believe about God is only a human construct. If we have spiritual humility, then we will acknowledge that God is greater than anything we can say about God and that all our faiths are flawed because they are all based on our incapability and incapacity to perceive the wholeness that is God. God is greater.

We should never confuse a system of beliefs with God. Accepting our limited human ability to know God means that we ought to respect our differences and our variations as the limited human creations they are. It means setting aside centuries of religious and ethnic intolerance; it means seeking to practice the ideals of our respective faiths and allowing others to do the same; it means finally learning to live and work together.

A Plea to Let God Be

In Hebrew, the word for God is *Elohim* or *El* or *Elo-ah*, all cognately related to the Arabic "Allah." But what does God—*Elohim*—mean? Strictly speaking, *Elohim* is not a name; it's a job title, and one that many ancient Near Eastern deities were given by their peoples.[2] But for Jews, God also has a personal name, several of them in fact.

In *Shemot* (*Exodus*) 3, in what is almost a humorous skit,[3] after encountering God in a talking Burning Bush, Moshe asks for God's name. Imagine Moshe's consternation when God replies "*Ehyeh-Asher-Ehyeh*," meaning "I am/will be who/what I am/will be." God tells Moshe to use that name when he speaks in God's

2. Thus, Ya'acov (Jacob) vows after his vision of the ladder that if YHVH will do "x" and "y" for him, then YHVH will be his *elohim* (god), the implication being that if YHVH fails to help him, then Yaakov is free to choose another, higher performing deity)—see *Bereisheet/ Genesis* 28:20-22.

3. In fact, Heller, in *God Knows*, made it a humorous skit. See pp. 33-35.

name to Paro (Pharaoh) and the Israelites. God also says to Moshe, "you may also call me '*Ehyeh*' ('I will be') for short." What a sense of humor! Imagine going up against the king of the greatest empire of its day and demanding: "Thus says '*I will be*,' let My people go." No wonder Moshe had trouble convincing Paro to do his bidding!

God has another, related name, comprised of the Hebrew letters "yud, hay, vav and hay," which may be rendered in English as "YHVH," and it is used throughout the Bible and in Jewish prayers to this day. Scholars call this name the Tetragrammaton, which is Greek for "four letters." In Jewish tradition YHVH is unutterable, both because it is believed to be God's holy, ineffable name, and because its pronunciation, which only the High Priest knew, was lost when the Temple was destroyed. Biblical scholars often pronounce it as Yahweh—but who knows? (Personally, I believe YHVH to be the sound of breath entering and leaving our bodies and should be "pronounced" accordingly: Yah, breathe in; Veh, breathe out.)[4]

When Jews see the letters "YHVH," we say "*Adonai*" meaning "LORD" and most Bible translations and Jewish prayer books follow this convention. Traditional Jews call YHVH "HaShem," which simply means "The Name." That name, YHVH, also has a special meaning of its own that says a great deal about the Jewish perception of God. The letters Y H V H represent a combination of the present and future tenses of the verb "to be." So, God's name is literally (and grammatically) pure potential: Is-ness; Will Be-ing; Shall Be.[5] But what does this mean?

The name YHVH suggests that God's essence is forward-looking and future-oriented, as in fact the Torah has God say by way of Self-description. After the Golden Calf fiasco, Moshe again asks to know God. But God says: "You cannot see My face, only My back"[6] meaning "You can only see where I've been, but that is not Me, for I am in movement, always in the present/future." Moshe is only allowed to view God's passing by, much as we might see the

4. See Michaelson, *Everything is God*, 47-49 for references to how other contemporary scholar/theologians discuss YHVH.

5. The latter pseudonym is suggested by Fishbane, in his profound book *Sacred Attunement*.

6. *Shemot/Exodus* 33:18-23.

81

wake of a ship without actually seeing the ship itself pass in front of us. It means that the Jewishly perceived God is always in a state of becoming. In other words, God is not yet whatever God will be; perhaps God is not perfect, but instead is in a state of on-going perfectibility.[7]

Traditionally, Judaism has accepted the premise that God is essentially unknowable.[8] Among classic medieval Jewish theologies, Maimonides' *via negativa*—using negative attributes to describe God—stands out as the most respectful way of expressing all we don't know about God. However, like any other religion, many philosophers and rabbis down through the ages spent much effort trying to define YHVH and to enshrine only certain perceptions of YHVH as legitimate, Maimonides included. But that effort, well-intentioned though it was, has resulted over time in ossified perceptions of God. Once any single perception of God is given the mantle of absolute truth, it becomes a humanly sanctified image—an idol, so to speak—for subsequent generations. As opposed to this, thinking of "God" as "YHVH" is the essence of the second of the Ten Utterances (Commandments): not to make any images of the divine. It keeps one's sense of God fresh—and a fresh God is a living God.

The name YHVH means that God is always beyond our limited abilities of comprehension, that God cannot be contained or controlled, summoned like a genie from a bottle or confined by our desire to define. We may think we know God in some way through past deeds attributed to God, or through our own experiences, but that should never constrain what God is, because God is ultimately a mystery, and God will be whatever God will be.

To exist is to change and to experience change. Dare we permit ourselves to say the same about God? Can God remain the same

---

7. For more on this interpretation, see Green, *Radical Judaism*. It also connects nicely with the God-concept of process theology.

8. Nonetheless, supremely pragmatic *for a religion*, Judaism basically says: "We can't really know anything concrete about YHVH, but we *do* know the way we are supposed to act because God gave us the commandments"—see *Devarim/Deuteronomy* 29:28 and 30:11-14, for example.

when we have not, either as peoples in history or as individuals?[9] Just as we are usually defined or known by our past deeds, so too we tend to define God by his purported, reported past deeds. But YHVH cannot be confined by the past. YHVH is present and future, so we need to let go of old theological concepts, even cherished, hallowed, time-honored concepts of "God" to let God be YHVH. We need the freedom to perceive God in our own ways, to reinvent God, as it were, for our own day and our own needs. What we are changing is not "God"; only our God-concepts. We are only admitting our collective, limited ability to "know God." Dare we assert "there is a God" while admitting that we haven't a clue about who/ what God is or what God does? Can we let "God" just be YHVH? Can we live with the idea of letting "God" simply BE?

Building a God-Concept

Once I got to this point in my thinking, I realized that it is not YHVH from whom I am seeking an explanation for suffering, but rather from my ancestors' perception of God that I inherited as a child and embraced as a young man. However, until I fully embraced YHVH's mystery, I stood spiritually conflicted, with part of me still clinging to traditional image of God and thus ready to argue and protest, and another part of me in the process of sloughing off this too-tight theological skin.

A Christian colleague, Daniel Migliore, once visited Seattle University as a scholar-in-residence and I found out that he and I were fellow travelers on a lonely theological road that advocates protest as a form of prayer. I confided that, despite my rejection of

---

9. Consider how later understandings of God in all the Abrahamic traditions, which view God as perfect, unchanging and omni-everything differ from those in the Bible. Reading the Tanach (Bible), we see no indication that God is perfect and unchanging. Instead, the Bible depicts God changing his mind, regretting some of his deeds, getting angry, and sometimes doing things that are downright disturbing, even scary. That is far from being perfect. The God the Abrahamic faiths share, conceived in the early centuries of the Common Era, is a far cry from the God depicted in the more ancient Jewish scriptures. The point is not that God changes, but that our conceptions of the divine do.

many of the accoutrements of the traditional God, I could not let completely go of this old supernatural God-concept of my ancestors. I was both wrestling with and releasing God at the same time and I was confused. "Anson," he said, "why do you need to resolve it? What's wrong with living with contradiction?" Ultimately his advice freed me up to move in new theological directions.

In the course of my spiritual development, I have moved away from the classical concept of a caring, supernatural God who intervenes in history and in individual human lives (the moved Mover) to a philosophically-based God who still intervenes (the unmoved Mover), to a deist concept of a God who exists, but does not intervene (the unmoved Unmover), and now am considering the possibility of a God who is empathetic but inactive (the moved Unmover). As I distinguish between YHVH and our human constructs of "God," I am forced to admit that I have ideas that I impose on YHVH's ineffability too and I find myself building a god-concept of my own.

What does my emerging god-concept look like?

As always, I start from the ground up, with what I experienced and what I believe to be real. From my most significant spiritual experience, I intuit that YHVH is somehow an actual Presence. But since I cannot verify this, I can only go so far as to say that I want, need, and even choose to conceive of God in this way.

Then, I acknowledge that my god-concept is built on the bedrock of primeval experiences of the divine. Our historical religions are the product of an ancient mindset in which God was perceived to speak directly to individuals and to act through natural and historical events. Their perceptions of the world and the divine-human relationship are different than ours.

It might help to understand this point by comparing our religions to the human developmental process. We all know that children process information differently and that they understand "God" and "faith" and other theological concepts differently than do adults.[10] Why not apply the same principle to our collective

10. See for example Fowler, *Stages of Faith.*

spiritual experiences and allow for change and growth over the millennia?

I am suggesting that our concepts of God represent a collective human developmental process akin to how each of us grows and learns. Paralleling a child's sense of faith, traditional religions have been based on the existence of a god or gods, who function as a supernatural parent (for better or worse). I think it is bred into our very beings, particularly at certain stages of individual life and at certain stages of civilization, to view God in this way. Thus, our ancient and revered holy texts tell us more about our ancestors' ideas of God and the world than they do of the mystery that is God. A rabbinic colleague, Rav Soloff, has delineated some of these stages as follows:

> When man's world was the size of a family, his creator and supreme authority, his God could be an ancestor. When man's world was his clan, his creator and supreme authority, his God could be a patriarch. When man's world was his nation, his creator and supreme authority, his God could be a king. And when vast empires arose to rule over scores of kingdoms, prophets came to believe that there was One God, the King of Kings . . .
>
> In most recent centuries man's astronomical world has exploded to encompass billions of years and myriads of universes, while his "tangible" world has imploded to infinitesimal particles and incomprehensible dimensions . . .
>
> In this new century "God" can no longer be imagined as the biblical Creator/King and Lawgiver/Savior, His Word revealed in human speech, never to be reinterpreted. God must be understood as Unlimited, beyond human imagination.[11]

11. Personal Communication. See also Soloff, "*My God,*" in *CCAR Journal*, Winter 1999. Another rabbinic colleague, Daniel Schiff, "*Reimagining Torah,*" in *CCAR Journal*, Summer 1994, 49–64 proposes a metaphor which sees "Torah as the early life development of the Jewish personality" noting that the Torah offers critical foundational knowledge that shapes how Jews see and feel the world, and it provides the earliest lessons regarding the primary relationships of self, family, and God. Still playing with the concepts of growth, development and relationship, but this time seeing them from God's perspective, as

The assumption that underlies all these diverse God-concepts, and which has sustained the Jewish people's faith down through the centuries, is that all these God-concepts represent One and the same Being, YHVH.[12] This same assumption also sustains Christianity, Islam and other faiths, and the various God-concepts each has developed and maintained over the centuries. All our ideas about the divine are interrelated; all are one—if we choose to see them as such—wheels within wheels, as Yehezkiel (Ezekiel) would say, and all part of a greater Whole.

Next, because I am a Jew, I *choose* to view God primarily through a Jewish lens. Beyond what I have imbibed from the well of Jewish tradition are ideas I have gleaned from the study of other faiths and through personal reflection. All these ideas influence my conception of "the living God," which occurs within the context of the North American Jewish relationship with God, which occurs within the context of the general North American religious experience, which occurs within the context of the late twentieth/early twenty-first century world religious experience. And my sense of YHVH also is simultaneously related to Jewish God-concepts of the European Enlightenment *and* to a Hasidic Jew's view of God in eighteenth-century Eastern Europe *and* a Chinese Jew's sense of God in the seventeenth-century; to a Sephardic Jew's conception of God in medieval Muslim Spain *and* a Judean's understanding of God in the first century of the common era *and* an ancient Israelite's perception of God in the fourth-century before the Common Era. All very different ways of looking at God, to be sure, but all somehow related, the earlier all influencing the latter, and all influencing me.

Because of my Jewish cultural context and my own personal preferences, if and when I choose to endow YHVH with any

---

it were, one could consider Torah to be the *Portrait of Yahweh as a Young God*, as the title of a book by Greta Wels-Schon puts it, or as Jack Miles describes in *God: A Biography*.

12. This assumption is indirectly affirmed in the Sh'ma, the core prayer of Judaism (which in fact is not a prayer at all, but a reminder): "Hear O Yisra-el, YHVH is our God, YHVH is One." While most people assume this to mean we worship only one God (who also happens to be the "true" God), it also asserts that all our various ways of conceiving God are one too: "Hear O Yisra-el, that Being we call YHVH is our God, all our ideas of YHVH are One."

qualities at all, they would be those qualities that Jews (and others) traditionally have believed God to have and which I still value, primarily because they are what I want to implement in my life and in this world: first and foremost, the attributes of justice and mercy, compassion, love, and accessibility. If I were building a god-concept that, miraculously, could become "God," I'd want to imbue my god with all these fine qualities.

At the same time, however, there are many other traditional qualities that trouble me, specifically those based around the concept of a supernatural God, a God who exists above, beyond, and outside Creation. Associated with this concept of a supernatural God are qualities that I reject as contrary to my experience, repugnant, or archaic. First and foremost, that God is omnipotent and omniscient; second, that God can intervene in history and/or in individual lives; third, images of God as male, a warrior, king, judge, punitive father, or husband; and fourth, peripherals such as the angelic court. These attributes may be no more or less valid than the ones I prefer. The only real difference is that these do not speak to me, mostly because my historical and cultural context is so different from the ones in which these attributes originally were developed.

All these attributes, based on the concept of a supernatural God, are a problem for me. They are a problem because of how petitionary prayer doesn't work; they are a problem because of unwarranted suffering in our world; they are a problem because a supernatural God belongs to an era in which the earth was at the center of the universe, as flat as a pancake, with the sky as a solid hemisphere above, and Heaven—with God enthroned—beyond that. In the beginning, this God and His hosts competed with the gods of other nations; then, having vanquished them, He derided them as idols; and finally, God and His Heavenly Host reigned supreme and unassailable for centuries until the modern era, when the scientific/philosophical assault on theism began. But, as John Shelby Spong has pointed out, theism and God are not the same.[13] Theism is but one way of looking at God and, in my opinion, its time is done. That "God" is "dead"; but YHVH is and shall be.

13. Spong, *Why Christianity Must Change or Die*, chapters 3 and 4.

I am troubled by the generally judgmental, male God imagery and gender bias that predominate in the Abrahamic traditions. But it is hard to say what bothers me more: the male authority-figure imagery or simply that imagery is used at all. Imagery is a problem, not just because it creates images in our minds and thus limits YHVH, but also because imagery is ambiguous. "God as Father" may constitute a loving, protective image for one person; a savage, brutal image for another.

These are precisely the same problems I also have with female imagery associated with God.[14] For me, describing YHVH with female imagery in addition to male ones only compounds the problem of using imagery in the first place. Both are equally offensive because they limit and confine our conceptions of YHVH. So, if I don't address God as Father, King, or Judge, I also won't address God as Mother or even by such gender-neutral terms as Parent or Ruler. The idea of God as father, mother or parent no longer works for me. Terms such as these are far more than I am willing or able to say about YHVH. Creator, I can live with.

Paradoxically, inanimate God imagery bothers me far less because no one is going to confuse God with being a Rock, a Light, a Fortress, etc. Everyone knows these are only metaphors. But, given my reticence to talk about God, I have no real need of appealing metaphors and similes with which to describe God. To describe YHVH in any way is a form of image-making and, as a radical monotheist, I prefer just to let YHVH Be. (Being an iconoclast is hell.)

The qualities traditionally ascribed to God bother me much less now because I know they are only human attributions of God,

14. In traditional Jewish religious thought, feminine images associated with God are all based on God being seen as "male." It should be noted that most of these feminine aspects are nouns with feminine endings in Hebrew, as if to say that their gender is predicated on their grammar. Some of the more common consorts are: the *Shekhinah*, or God's feminine Presence that dwells on earth (paralleling God, our Father in Heaven); *Shabbat*, the Sabbath Queen or Bride, a personification of the seventh day; *Hochmah*, a personification of Wisdom; Torah, not just the book but a metaphysical entity that God consulted in creating the world; *Yisrael*, the personification of the Jewish people, married to God; and *Yerushalayim /Tziyyon*, personifications of Jerusalem and the Land of Zion.

our projections onto YHVH, not actually YHVH. I have also "for-given" God for all that has been and still is wrong in our world. In other words, I have let go of traditional perceptions of "God" and let go of the issue of divine providence to let God simply be YHVH.

Nonetheless, when my friend, the late Mary Dougherty, de-scribed her vision of the divine-human relationship as: "God as she, a mother or—even better—a grandmother, who has created us, reared us, given us role models (like Jesus) and set us on our col-lective and individual ways; and now that we are grown up, really wants us to succeed, and grieves with and for us when we don't," I have to admit to a certain deeply-felt longing. My heart yearns for such an intimate sense of connection and relationship with God as she describes; my head, however, says that this imagery presumes far too much. To keep the peace between my body parts, I listen to both and strive to be content living with this contradiction until, if ever, I know differently.

Finally, I come to the core of my god-concept. Based on my personal experience, I feel YHVH's omnipresence is real—it is the only "omni" I accept—precisely because I experienced it. I expect *nothing* of YHVH other than to be aware of YHVH's presence, and this feels right for me. I am willing to let God just be the Name, YHVH, the One who will be what the One will be. The One who is experienced.

I feel that YHVH is somehow present everywhere and in ev-erything, and a bit of that Presence resides in every living person, animating every living creature and even, perhaps, our entire planet as well. Because I view Creation, not as a machine, but as organisms within organisms, worlds within worlds, a living whole, I choose to think that YHVH somehow both infuses everything with "the breath of life" and at the same time transcends everything with "Presence."[15] (I say this without knowing exactly what I mean, but I do intuit it.) Scholars call this conception of God "panentheism" and, although it is only a theological concept, not reality, it appeals

15. See *Tehillim/Psalms* 139:7–8; *Yermiyahu/Jeremiah* 23:24; *Yeshiyahu/Isaiah* 66:1.

to me, in part because it allows me to retain and build upon the foundations of my people's sacred stories and traditions.[16]

What I am able to affirm is that, based on the name YHVH, "God" represents the infusion of constant creativity—pure positive potentiality—into the world, which in turn gives all living things the possibility and the power to live and grow—and, yes, to decline and die—both individually and collectively. YHVH is the animating force of all life; the living dynamic of all that exists; the source both of what we perceive as good and what we perceive as bad. Based on my experience, I feel that YHVH can be experienced and, if one is open to it, one is able—occasionally for certain and ideally continually—to tap into the sensations of peace, love and joy that derive from that connection.

Being alert to the presence of YHVH in life means seeing the "Presence" everywhere and in everything. I see all life as an extension of YHVH because life is the perpetual re-creation of new possibilities, or potentialities. In the natural world, this process apparently is neither good nor bad, it is simply life growing and adapting in seemingly endless variation of itself, like the growth that goes on in our own bodies with our cells replacing themselves continuously, oblivious to our conscious existence and will.

Having an awareness of this "Presence" means, at the very least, that when I look at other living things, I strive to recognize the existence of a shared divine dimension. They are no less than we: unique particles, or moments, of life's slow unfolding. Based on this principle alone, we ought to treat other living creatures with a degree of reverence, even those we choose to eat.

I also see YHVH's presence in each individual's maturation process. That which begins at birth is the potential for good: for growth, for improvement, and for development. This process is manifested when one sees loved ones grow from oblivious infancy to the point when they can interact with other people, when they reach out with the all the sweet innocence that only the very young have and begin to build actual relationships with those around

---

16. See Green, *Seek My Face, Speak My Name*, Borg, *God We Never Knew*, and Bass, *Grounded*. Spong, in *Why Christianity Must Change or Die*, calls his non-theistic God "the Ground of Being."

them. This positive exercise of potentiality is observed when youth seizes hold of maturity and ventures out into the world; when two people find love together; when a baby is born; and when we care for one another, even to the point of death and beyond. All these are positive acts of growth and development.

I think this exercise of divine potentiality is more consciously applied in human creativity, from commonplace simple things like how we dress ourselves or how we decorate our dwellings to the grander outbursts of creative expression as when an artist plays with color and shape, or when a musician builds sound upon sound, or when a writer weaves words into narratives or poetry. But as much as I value human creativity as a divine revelation of sorts, I think that this divine presence, this power of positive potentiality, resides most particularly in our doing good deeds.

To be sure, my soul stirs to the idea of a God who somehow actually shares our fate and participates in our journeys,[17] and I realize that to hold this belief could be very comforting. Knowing that somehow God shares what we are going through when we feel distress can fuel our inner spiritual reserves, enabling us to struggle along with renewed energy. Having such a God would also pass my Holocaust litmus test because such a God could be a source of personal comfort and support in Auschwitz but without the expectation that God would actively intervene. But I cannot say with certainty that God suffers when we do, or that God celebrates or is energized when we choose a higher, nobler path in our actions. YHVH may somehow "care" (to put it in human terms) or may somehow "participate" in what we do, but I don't really *know* this to be the case. All I know is that I experienced a benign—dare I say loving—Presence. So, I set this idea of an empathic God aside

17. In both Judaism and Christianity, it is taught that God somehow shares our pain and that what we do "affects" God. This empathic, suffering but ultimately active God is as much a traditional Jewish concept of God as it is obviously a Christian one. In some *midrashim*, God feels pain when Israel suffers in Exile, mourns, weeps, acts as one who is ill, even is led into exile with his people. See p. 83 of *Arguing with God* and texts referenced there. Also consider this beautiful teaching from the Zohar: "In all deeds it behooves a person to imitate the celestial model, and to realize that according to the nature of a deed below there is a responsive stirring on high." (*Zohar Bamidbar* 118a/b).

CHOOSING LIFE AFTER TRAGEDY

even as I yearn to know it is real. Perhaps someday I may be blessed with this knowledge; perhaps not—but it is not something I am currently willing to take on faith.[18]

A Presence, perhaps with a *hint* of personality, who/that provides potentiality to life—*this* is a job description for a deity?! Not by many people's standards, but it works for me. YHVH is there to be experienced, not to do our bidding, and that is why I assert: "I know there is a God, I just don't know what S/He/It does." Nowadays, I rarely choose to speak about "God." It is just too confusing a term. When people ask me if I believe in God, I say, "Tell me what you mean by 'God' and what you mean by 'believe' and I'll try to answer your question." Rather, I prefer to follow Lao Zi's dictum: "Those who know do not speak; those who speak do not know."

18. The founder of Multifaith Works, my mentor, the late Rev. Gwen Beighle, who worked with many people dying from AIDS related issues and also had to cope with her own terminal ovarian cancer, taught: "Psalm 23 says: 'Yea though I walk through the valley of the shadow of death I will fear no evil, for You are with me.' It does not say that we will not suffer. But it does say that, as we go through suffering, God is somehow present with us to comfort us. Knowing this can help us accept what is happening." This view of God amid suffering worked for Gwen, who modeled how one can overcome a tragic situation to die with grace and dignity, faith and hope. Hers was the most peaceful dying I ever was privileged to witness. I can only hope to die as good a death, even if I don't share her faith (yet).

Chapter 12

Unraveling Revelation

A Different Understanding of Revelation

IN THE ABRAHAMIC FAITHS, it is impossible to separate the issue of suffering and the role of God without discussing the matter of divine revelation because revelation is the quintessential act of divine intervention in human affairs. Having severed the connection between God and suffering by changing my understanding of God, I want to briefly discuss revelation, not only for reasons of consistency but also because it opens the door to how we can best deal with our own suffering and that of others.

Revelation is such a challenging concept! Consider, for example, the words that introduce so many biblical commandments, "And YHVH spoke to Moshe, saying"—and specifically the word "saying." Think about it: What does this word, so commonly and frequently used in the Bible with reference to God, actually mean? With no larynx, lips or tongue, how does God speak? And if it was not speech as we know it, how did Moshe "hear" these non-words? And how, then, did these non-words become words? And whose words were they? How much was God's revelation and how much was Moshe's (or someone else's) extrapolation? Perhaps God communicated through a dream or by a vision, or perhaps it was an inner voice projected externally?

Let me state at the outset that I do not now believe the revelation to Moshe or any other prophet was supernatural. The problem with a supernatural revelation is that *if* revelation is a miraculous intervention by God into the normal course of human events, *then* there is a basic—and for me unacceptable—contradiction between this phenomenon and the world of experience. It is exactly the same problem I have with linking God and suffering.

For me, any given revelation must be viewed from the ground up. A revelation is one individual's particular and creative response to what s/he perceives or discerns to be God's call in a specific situation. This is what I learned from studying the Kaifeng Jewish synthesis of Jewish and Chinese theologies.

I do no disservice to the messenger or the message when I assert that revelation is a human response to a perceived experience of the divine. What matters in the end is that the revelatory experience transformed the messenger and resulted in his/her transmitting something of profound, life-changing importance to the people of his/her time and to humanity ever after. If you acknowledge that revelations are limited by time and place yet also that they resonate with value and meaning, then they still retain much of their worth as "timeless" teachings—"God's own words" as it were.

But what we call the Bible are revelations' remnants cobbled together and written down by human hands.[1] How much simpler it would be if we considered our various holy texts as products of particular times and places. We would feel much freer about how we evaluate various stories and commandments even though we could still regard the texts as repositories of great insight, which also have been imbued with the additional wisdom of subsequent generations. But however divinely inspired we may think them to be, they are nonetheless human documents evincing attitudes about God and society from ancient times!

I now view the Jewish holy books as testaments to the continuing and evolving encounter—or, as the name "Yisrael" suggests, the on-going struggle—of the Jewish people to relate to its perceptions of God, YHVH. As of this writing, the collective

---

1. See Fishbane, *Text and Texture*, xiii.

Jewish experience is about 4,000 years in the making and Torah probably has been told, adapted, recorded, interpreted, and commented upon for at least 3,000 of those years. That we have such an ancient sacred text, that it is accompanied by several millennia of commentary representing the best wisdom of the ages, testifies to the power of the mystery that lies at its heart. And that is why I too continue to mine the Torah for insights that give meaning, purpose, and value to my life.

Antiquity has bestowed an ever-increasing holiness to our holy books and when a text assumes near-divine status itself then, in many religious traditions, it becomes blasphemous to suggest that the events and laws in their holy texts ever happened otherwise.[2] And once they have been enshrined as religious truths, they also serve as a foundation for the institutional religious edifices built upon them. In the end, the texts and the institutions end up being as sanctified as the root experience/ revelation that initially galvanized their creation.[3]

2. Over the centuries, we Jews have emerged not only as long-time monotheists but also as long-time bibliolators, or Book-worshippers. We may have given "God" to the world, but we kept a tighter clasp on the Torah. The physical Torah scroll and the presence of God became all but synonymous in Jewish worship. Furthermore, the same principle of sanctity eventually was applied to the Talmud and even to the prayer book. It was not for nothing that Muslims called us the "People of the Book."

3. Nor are we today immune from this tendency to sanctify documents. Consider the American Constitution. Like the Torah, the Constitution is valued because its origin goes back to America's very beginnings; it defines America both for Americans and for other nations. As with Torah, constitutional scholars sometimes attempt to determine—but are just projecting their views onto—the intent of the Founding Fathers. Consider also how we revere and preserve the physical document known as the Constitution. It is the modern equivalent of storing the Tablets of the Law in the Temple! Imagine how the Constitution and the Founding Fathers who drafted it will be regarded in, say, 1000 or 2000 years. Jill Lepore draws the comparison between constitutional originalists and Christian fundamentalist readings of the Bible, and contrasts those who view the Constitution as a human document with those who enshrine it as divinely inspired, in her article "The Commandments."

The Relativity of Revelation

For Jews, Sinai is the quintessential revelatory experience. According to the Torah itself, Moshe and people received both *mitzvot* (commandments) and a revelatory experience.[4] But who received what and how much? Inquiring rabbinic minds wanted to know.

The ancient rabbis discussed which of the 613 commandments God gave directly to the entire people. One *midrash* stated that every Jew at Sinai heard the Torah being given in a distinct and personal way: young men one way, old men another; women a third way, and children a fourth—even the yet-to-be-born heard it in a special way.[5] Another *midrash* asserted that God gave the Big Ten, and Moshe the remaining 603. Yet another suggested that God gave the first two of the Ten alone and Moshe the remainder,[6] because if one affirms the first two, then all the rest follow; but if one cannot accept the first two commandments, then the whole Covenant falls apart. Ultimately, in rabbinic thinking, the revelation came to include not only the entire Written Torah (both the commandments and the narrative text) but also the Oral Torah (later rabbinic interpretations and adaptations).

However, centuries later, and from a totally different part of the world, there came a profound—and perhaps humorously playful— Hasidic commentary that elaborates a more mystic interpretation. This particular Hasidic teaching states that God directly uttered *only* the first letter of the first commandment—an *aleph*—a letter that just happens to be a silent letter![7] How many words are contained in that enunciated silence? For me, this teaching confirms what I think revelation is all about: It has to do with experiencing YHVH being present; it's not about content.

4. There is some discrepancy between the accounts of *Shemot/Exodus* 20:15-18 and *Devarim/Deuteronomy* 5:19-28.

5. *Shemot/Exodus Rabbah* 5:9

6. *Babylonian Talmud*, Makkot 24a and Horayot 8a..

7. My teacher Arthur Lagawier first shared this teaching with me. He probably learned it from his Hasidic grandfather. It originated with Rabbi Mendl Torum of Rymanov, a Hasidic master. His comment is based on the *Zohar* (II:85b), which states that this "aleph" contained the whole Torah. See Green, *Seek My Face, Speak My Name*, 115-117.

If revelation is an experience of the divine presence, and the content is something human beings add subsequently, then it is important to differentiate between the two.[8] By separating the experience from the content, we can both "free" God from the chains of past perceptions and look at the content of a revelation more objectively.

Traditionally, different faiths have transformed the revelatory experience into content, either primarily as commandments (in the case of Judaism), or belief (in the case of Christianity based on Paul's vision of Jesus), or both (in the case of Islam). Just as Judaism differentiated itself from the religions of Egypt and Canaan, so too, as Christianity and Islam developed, each in turn asserted its claim to supersede its predecessor as God's chosen, while its predecessor denounced the new faith as fallacy. But why would God need to update revelation from time to time? One revelation ought to have been enough. However, if one considers revelation from the human side, then there is always a need for revision and reform, because the receptor and implementer is a limited creature made of flesh and blood, here today and gone tomorrow. Our experiences perpetually call out for new understandings of what we think God "asks" of us.

If the revelatory experience is a sort of spiritual insight or enlightenment, then it all depends on one's aptitude, preparation, expectations, level of spiritual development and the lens through which one looks at life. Each perception is unique, distinct and valid, but all represent all too human responses to a revelatory experience of some kind. Our understandings of the ultimate reality and of our place in the universe complement one another, precisely because that reality is ultimately unknowable and the infinite whole will always be greater than the sum of its many parts. Indeed, every faith tradition "hears God" in unique and distinct ways.

8. I'm in good company in making this differentiation. Franz Rosenzweig wrote that "the Lord spoke" signifies the end of revelation and the beginning of interpretation while Abraham Joshua Heschel viewed the Torah as "a minimum of revelation and a maximum of interpretation." See Sommer, *Revelation and Authority*.

This perception applies not just to my contemporaries, but also to those writers and doers of deeds in many lands and in many ages, of many faiths and many cultures. All our perceptions are One, transcending time and place, different though they may be. Our ideas of God, our religious civilizations, our understanding of our obligations, indeed our very lives, are like a coral. We, the living, represent the uppermost tip of a great reef that grows continually, building upon the concepts of previous generations and adding our own ideas to their foundation before we too pass away. There is no progress in this metaphor; only one generation building on the perceptions and lives of its predecessors while reaching toward the light.

I think that the solution to the conflicting claims of our different faiths lies first in distinguishing religion from the spiritual experience. The former ought to be seen as a *particular* cultural expression of a *universal* human experience, which is the latter. Our religions are the distinctive clothing we wear over our naked human spirituality. Because revelation is a human response to a perceived divine call, then myriad responses are possible.[9] They can be as diverse as our languages, as multiple as there are people.

Once I had let go of my inherited perceptions of God and my too parochial view of revelation, I found I could engage with people of other faiths in a more genuine way. If we are all viewing different facets of the same divine gemstone and if all our faiths are cultural trappings laid upon our naked spirituality, then what is the point in arguing about whose revelation is truer or whose religious civilization is wiser, greater or better? If revelation really is about experiencing the ineffable, then accepting this premise conceivably can make our faiths less exclusivist and more appreciative of one another's experiences. More importantly, it allows us to look for shared values that we can use to overcome suffering.

---

9. Rabbi Shmuel Eliezer Edeles (Eastern Europe, 1555–1631) taught that the entire nation of 600,000 people received the Torah at Sinai to teach that the Torah has (at least) 600,000 possible interpretations. And if we have so many possible interpretations in just one faith, how much the more so when we consider all our faiths and all humanity?

The great scandal of the Abrahamic faiths has been their intolerance not only of non-monotheistic faiths, but also of each other and of internal dissent, because revelation brooked no competing views. Over the centuries, our religious differences have obscured our religious similarities, leading to discrimination, persecution, wars, much death, and needless suffering.[10] We need to make a break with how we have conducted ourselves previously. Perhaps, as with children and parents, religions must separate one from another and grow apart as they develop their own unique messages and accomplishments, but it is a shame and often a horror to see how we have dealt with this process throughout history.

Casting blame for these tragedies is pointless—it is easy to do but so harmful for future relations. The past does have power in the present, but we are not doomed to repeat the past. Each occasion inherits history but also a moment of divine potentiality—an opportunity to let go, forgive, change, and grow—and this can enable us to transcend our pasts.

Only then we can begin to build relationships that are new and filled with potential for improvement. By recognizing our human limitations in the knowledge of God, by acknowledging our multiple perspectives on "God," and by placing responsibility for the well-being of humanity squarely on our collective shoulders, we can set the stage for human reconciliation, interfaith harmony, spiritual growth and the healing of our world. The proof of one's connectedness with the divine lies in living lives of practical spirituality. Theology aside, it is not that complicated.

10. For a significant book about religious extremism and its vile fruits in the world, see Sacks, *Not in God's Name*. Two wonderful condemnations of religion, specifically the Abrahamic ones, are by the so-called New Atheists: Harris, *End of Faith* and Hitchens, *God Is Not Great*.

Chapter 13

Two Experiences of Compassion

I'D LIKE TO SHARE two experiences, one uplifting and one over-whelming, which were transformational moments in understanding of the role of compassion in my life.

One year, as I was about to lead High Holy Day services, I looked out over the assembled people and saw several hundred individuals sitting before me. In the brief moment that it took, I suddenly grew aware of the fact that each of these people brought with them to this service a lifetime's worth of experiences. Here were all these beings, each with thoughts and feelings tucked away deep inside, yet simulta-neously here were those same hidden things, floating like comic strip thought-bubbles above each person's head. I felt overwhelmed by the cacophony of all these lives, each with their private joys and secret sorrows, their silent fears and unspoken expectations.

At that moment, I was struck with a profound sense of compas-sion for everyone, myself included, for our physical and emotional limitations, for our ineptitude, for our valiant efforts and for our fail-ings; and I thought "Perhaps this is how God feels about us—like the parent of a toddler, who cannot but shake his head at the little one's attempts to cope with life."

I was struck with the thought the Abrahamic faiths envision a deity who alone can break through the barriers that separate us, one from the other; who can see into our souls, even into places where we ourselves are not honest enough or brave enough to look; who can relate to each of us, in our totality, yet who has energy to spare for all Creation; and that this conception of God is wonderful because this God so precisely transcends our most basic existential limitation: our sense of separateness. In that moment, I wished that, if this God did exist, He would come and heal us of all our secret wounds!

All this only took a few seconds and then the sensation passed. It was time to lead my congregation in prayer. And so, we began. . .but I never felt the same towards a group of people again without having a moment of compassion for them all, myself included.

This was the beginning of my acquiring wisdom: don't be judgmental; have a little compassion (*rochmoness*, in Yiddish) for other people. As sweet as this experience was, the second experience its opposite, a spiritually and emotionally painful moment when the proverbial straw broke the camel's (i.e., my) back:

The evening that the doctor told me that my wife would have to undergo serious emergency surgery for her abdominal obstruction coincided with the first anniversary of my father's death. The latter event, called a yahrzeit *in European Jewish tradition, is a significant annual occasion in Jewish mourning rituals. Emotional as it is, that* yahrzeit *was especially so because it was my first.*

Since my father had died suddenly the year before, I had kept a picture of him on display for comfort. That day, I left the hospital to come home, freshen up, light the memorial candle, and recite the traditional kaddish *prayer. But as I gazed at his image, I was overwhelmed with sadness and despair for all that had happened: the deaths of my brother-in-law and sister-in-law, my aunt and uncle; my wife's cancer, my mother's dangerous heart condition, my father's dropping dead, our daughter's recurring leukemia, and now my wife's emergency surgery.*

As others before me have done, I sought to ease my pain, not in prayer to God, but in alcohol. At first, I took a drink to salute my dad's memory—which was ironic because he was almost a teetotaler. I wept as I recalled that I had not been able to bid him farewell because he had died so suddenly. Nor had I been able to mourn my father as I had wanted to, according to Jewish ways: I had had to leave the shiva, *the seven-day initial mourning period, in Toronto, to fly back home to Seattle, to be with my wife while she underwent chemotherapy in the hospital; I had been unable to attend the unveiling of my father's tombstone because our daughter was hospitalized with leukemia; and now I was unable to be in Toronto again for the first* yahrzeit *because my wife was about to undergo emergency abdominal surgery. And I was scared out of my mind about that! As I sat there lamenting and crying, I kept on drinking.*

Grief had isolated me, even without my being aware of it. I had seduced myself into being "the family strong one," and I felt I had no one to turn to. I couldn't bother my wife, who was in the hospital; I didn't want to upset our children more than they already were; I didn't want to disrupt our friends' holiday plans with my misery. I felt utterly alone.

Fortunately, even in her drugged-out state, my wife knew that something was amiss. She told several visiting friends that she thought I needed a shoulder to lean on, and they told several others, and before too long I was enveloped in lovingkindness. At first, I resisted. "I am strong," I said. "I am fine. My wife needs support, not me." But down deep, I knew they were right, so I opened up and began to talk. Yes, I had been the strong one for my family, but even the strong have feelings, and we had been—were still going through—quite an ordeal. So, I talked, not just to friends and family, but also to a therapist and, in due time, in a grief group. Gradually I regained my emotional and spiritual equilibrium, but it was an incredibly painful time.

Because of my work and my studies, I thought I was prepared to handle the experience of suffering. And initially I was. But suffering and grief come not all at once, they are more like breaking waves, coming one after another, pounding on the breakwater of one's inner reserves, overwhelming them when one least expects it. Mishlei (Proverbs) 9:10 says, "The *yir'at* of YHVH is the beginning of wisdom." Curiously, the Hebrew word for "awe" and "fear" is one and the same. Although I knew by now that "God" was not responsible for our travails, the number of crises we had endured brought me to the awe/fear of the random terror of disease and death in our lives.

From this low point in my life, I learned two significant lessons and I hope that, unlike calculus, they stay with me the rest of my days. First, I learned to expect the unexpected, to let go of my plans and to live as fully as I can by seizing the moment. There is a Yiddish proverb that goes, "Man plans and God laughs." We all tend to spend life planning for the future, presuming that life is predictable. But it ain't—ever. We just like to delude ourselves. Although it is important to have dreams for the future and equally important to plan for them, one also must remain unattached to them and let life run its uncharted course. I have learned again and again and again, to try to live in the present, to grab joy and celebrate life in whatever possible way I could. Even in the direst of times, I could find joy, for example, in looking at my wife's face as she rested, or in our holding hands. There is an exquisite feeling, both wondrous and painful, which accompanies an awareness of life's preciously short duration. Would that I could maintain that feeling at all times.

Second, even though I often had preached about "building a community of compassion" during the eleven years I served as Multifaith Works' director, I had never experienced it personally. I learned that, when one is in need, a community of compassion of some sort will often materialize to provide a personal safety net for that person.[1] That support may come from family or friends; or it may not. It can also come from total strangers who are present simply because they care. But for it to happen, one has to take a risk; one has to risk being vulnerable; one has to ask for support. One has to trust.

---

1. One can plan for this in advance. See Gibson and Pigott, *Personal Safety Nets.*

Chapter 14

Life is Good; Life is Growth

BEGINNING IN THE SUMMER of 2009, I had the opportunity to serve as the interim rabbi for a young Seattle congregation, Kol HaNeshamah. This would be my first full-time pulpit experience in my career in the thirty years since I was ordained! Intellectually, emotionally, and spiritually, I finally was ready to try working in the congregational field. And for a year—how bad could it be?

To my delight, I found the experience fulfilling and transforming. Where previously I had been too conflicted to lead the community in prayer, now I felt somewhat comfortable; where previously I felt too immature and inexperienced to counsel anyone, now I felt I had some real-life wisdom to back me up; and where previously I had intellectually raw ideas to offer, now I felt I had something personally genuine to share.

My newer ideas regarding prayer and suffering, God and life, seemed to resonate positively with many of my congregants. Did I need their validation of my ideas? In a way I did. As a rabbi and teacher, I had always entertained the hope that the spiritual struggle in which I had been engaged for so many years would somehow be of value to other people as they dealt with life's challenges. And it seemed that in this I was successful.

About two-thirds of the way through my year there, my wife, Merrily, was suddenly diagnosed with metastasized ovarian cancer in her spleen. It was news we had never expected to hear since we had been assured years ago that her first bout with cancer had ended in a rout of those deadly, disruptive cells.

The shock of my wife's having terminal cancer contributed greatly to my decision to move on. I needed a job that allowed me physical time and emotional space to be at home with her as much as possible. As we struggled to cope with our radically changing life situation, I began revisiting many of the ideas I had been working on in this book. I found that the still tentative conclusions I had reached really worked for me—although they did nothing to assuage my grief.

At the end of my interim year, I took jobs with Jewish Family Service and Kline Galland Hospice that offered me great flexibility and left me with the time and energy necessary to take care of my wife (and myself and the rest of our family). For many months we lived suspended in a realm of anxious unknowing, since we did not know how long she would live or how soon she would die. Some days we grieved; some days we laughed; but every day we tried to savor our time together. Usually, we don't have someone telling us that we are terminally ill (which we all are) to make us aware of life's true and oh-so-ephemeral preciousness. The irony is, of course, that this is how life should be lived regardless.

One day during my wife's final months, while sitting in the woods near our house, I began to think back once again to that formative spiritual experience I had had many decades earlier. For years, it had been the foundation of my belief in the existence of "God." Initially, I had simply connected my experience with the God of my ancestors, assuming the two were the same. (And as two experiences of the same mystery, one ancient and one modern, they were.) But it was an assumption on my part, and it took me years to unlink the two, to let go of the tyranny of my ancestors' perception of God and allow my own to evolve. My sense of God changed and grew just as I have matured, so perhaps I should say that my sense of God continues to evolve.

As I was meditating on this formative experience, it suddenly occurred to me that perhaps my experience was as much about "life" as it was about "God." After all, the key sensation had been the simultaneous awareness of my uniqueness and infinitesimal-ness—of unity and distinctness—even while I felt a benign Presence and an over-whelming sense of the intrinsic goodness and beauty of everything.

And then, sitting there in those woods, I felt it once again: a sensation of a "Creating and Sustaining Presence" that seemed to suffuse all life, wrapping everything in its embrace. I intuited that this "Presence" and "Life" went together hand-in-hand. They were one and basically good, even though bad things happened, and indeed were happening in our family. And at that moment, I accepted the fact that Merrily was going to die, that it was her time even if it wasn't according to our timetable, and that somehow I would survive the grief and pain I was about to suffer.

One cannot deny the reality of grief. It just has to be lived through and slowly integrated into your being until hopefully you re-emerge somewhat healed and somewhat whole (and always somewhat broken). But life will go on and that is good.

Life *is* good; it is growth, and it will always find a way to persevere. I see it in plants cracking through cement or worming their way around boulders towards the light. I have seen it when vegetation and animal life return after cataclysmic disasters, whether natural and man-made. I have witnessed it as Holocaust survivors choose to raise families and build new lives rather than give in to despair and suicide. And I have observed it in myself, a grieving man who, along with his family, remains in the process of rebuilding his life minus the presence of many loved ones.

In my case, as a hospice chaplain working first with dying people and then with grieving families, participating in a grief support group, and receiving one-on-one counseling, all of these helped me in my grieving process. But despite all this, I might have remained stuck much longer in serious despair and depression had not Richelle appeared, whether serendipitously or providentially (we disagree on this point), to warm my numbed soul with her sweet and caring presence, which enabled me to re-embrace life and love once again.

Life as I See It

One of the realities of life, it seems to me, is that although we need intimate relationships nonetheless, most of the time, we are not truly capable of transcending our physical and emotional distinctiveness. We also make the journey through life's stages on our own, individually—although we do like to compare notes. Just as parents cannot spare their children from falling as they learn to walk, so too we all must discover life's experiences, personally, for ourselves.

As we live, we learn that loss and grief are natural parts of human existence—would that it were otherwise—but they are as much a part of life as joy and pleasure. From the moment of birth until the day of death, life is made up of innumerable minor losses and a number of great ones, each with its own special grief, just as it is also made of innumerable gains, each with its own special joy. Ultimately, life ends, and with it all that we held dear. As much as we know that death is the inevitable conclusion of life, even so there is always a shocking sense of loss and a feeling of bewildered abandonment when it actually occurs.

So how did I deal with the fact that life itself ultimately entails separation from those about whom we care the most and the loss of all that we cherish? After many years of study and personal growth, I have arrived at a paradoxical synthesis of sorts: Life is suffering, just as the Buddha taught, and so I seek a general transcendence of my attachments to things and relationships, but then I remind myself, as my Jewish heritage affirms, that life is good, so I also seek engagement with all that life has to offer, and relationships above all.

Live as if Today Were the Last Day
of the Rest of Your Life

Judaism is remarkably non-dogmatic regarding the after-death and over the centuries Jews have postulated many things.[1] But even with

---

1. Jews at one time or another have advocated a shadowy netherworld (*Sheol*); transmigration of the soul (*gilgul ha-nefesh*); an immortal soul that returns to God (*hayyei olam*); and most normatively, belief in a personal physical resurrection after the coming of the Messiah and the Day of Judgment

all this speculation, the focus of the faith has always been on the here-and-now because how one lived here determined what came after, whatever the after-here is.

Perhaps this very diversity of ideas led me to realize, early on, that what was being taught went far beyond our ability to actually know. Since whatever might exist after death *is* beyond our knowing, all ideas of the after-death *are* just ideas—images, dreams, wish fulfillment—requiring giant leaps of faith. But what we really about the after-death know is *bupkis* (Yiddish for "nothing")!

However, all this is beside the point. Knowing that there is a time limit to all we do and love, we may better learn to cherish our time on earth. On Yom Kippur—a symbolic taste of death and the Day of Judgment according to Jewish tradition—we ask forgiveness first and foremost of ourselves and then of our fellow human beings and finally of God, for wasting time, for losing sight of that which is truly important in life. Yom Kippur and the preceding ten days are designed to help us get in touch with our mortality, to help get us back on track, to return to the Way, to try to do good better.

One of the most common attributes of the traditional God concept is God's presumed ability to know the innermost secrets of our hearts. Consequently, a dying person traditionally would believe that God would be looking at their deeds with an honesty we ourselves often lack, looking at the totality of who we are without the subjectivity that each of us has. Regardless of whether one believes in such a God, nonetheless we might do well to take stock of our lives *as if* there were such a God, who sees through our transparent devices and self-serving deceptions, *as if* there were an actual Day of Judgment after death.

In my work with people who were dying of AIDS, we tried our best to help these individuals make peace with the course their lives have taken. This process, if one is fortunate, may include having the actual opportunity to reconcile with family and friends, with oneself, and with one's God. Reconciliation means recognizing that however good one has been in life, one always falls short of perfection. Acknowledging this fact and asking forgiveness for one's

(*tehiyyat ha-meitim*).

shortcomings is an essential part of this reconciliation process. The Rev. Gwen Beighle called this "dying a good death" and later, she herself modeled just what she had so often talked about.

The nice part about dying a good death is that one need not wait until one is on one's deathbed to do it. Long ago, Rabbi Eliezar told his disciples, "Repent one day before your death," to which his students then asked, "Does a person know on what day he will die; that he should know when to repent?" And to which the sage responded, "All the more that you should repent today lest you die tomorrow."[2]

In Hebrew, the word for "repentance" is "*teshuvah*," but more literally it means "returning"—returning to walk along the path of God's instruction (Torah). The process of returning, of *teshuvah*, begins with a profound awareness of life and of death, with a sense of the preciousness of passing time and the need to reorder one's priorities.[3]

So, when Rabbi Eliezar says, "Repent one day before your death," he means that we should strive every day to live our lives with the same intensity as if we knew it was our last. Imagine how our lives would be if we chose to live each day as if it were the *last* day of the rest of our lives. We would be more focused on our relationships, more willing to forgive minor trespasses and perhaps even larger offenses too, more understanding of human foibles, more disposed to talk about things that really matter.

For Jews, death is not the annihilator of all meaning, rather it is an enhancer of meaning. When facing issues of life and death, business success or failure, squabbles between spouses, siblings and friends, all become less important. Because, when confronting the

2. *Babylonian Talmud*, Shabbat 153a. Rabbi Eliezar ben Hyrcanus lived at end of the first century and beginning of the second century of the Common Era.

3. This analysis is called "*heshbon hanefesh*," an accounting of one's soul. Ideally it is done continually, but at least annually during the month of Ellul and Ten Days of Return between Rosh Hashanah and Yom Kippur, and finally in the days or hours before one's death. My friend Bruce Kochis pointed out to me that teshuvah need not be drastic; not an 180° turn but something less also is fine. He joked that 180 is 10% of 180° and that is a good amount of change to aim for since "18" in Hebrew numerically represents "life."

merest possibility of death, you focus on the fragility and preciousness of life and your priorities get instantly rearranged for the better.

Any day can be a good day to die. There will always be more to
do, more to accomplish, and more milestones to reach. There may
be better or worse times to die in terms of its impact on your life
plan or on loved ones, but it is always a good day to die—particularly if you are ready to depart with "a good name."

How does one acquire a "good name"? According to Jewish
tradition, by the deeds we do and the way we behave. What matters
in the end are the acts of kindness and the love that is shown to
those whom we meet on life's path: family, friend and stranger alike.
It's what we hope to leave behind when we depart this life, secure
in the knowledge that we have contributed positively in some small
or large way towards improving life on this planet, so that when
people recall you, they will say "May his/her memory be for a blessing," meaning that people will recall the good you strove to do in
life and be motivated to act in a similar way. The epitaph of baseball
great Jackie Robinson reads: "A life is important only for the impact
it has on other lives." That is worth remembering and acting upon!

All these reflections came to me gradually as I processed my
grief and grieved my loss, from its inception with Merrily's terminal
cancer to her days of dying to her death to my dealing with my
loss, from the seven-day mourning period of *shiva* to the month-
long reduced mourning period *(hodesh)* to her *yahrzeit* (death
anniversary) and every day since. But, once I got over the darkest
of dark days when I despaired even of living without my beloved
companion, I slowly came back to the land of the living and to the
realization that, even with her being gone, life was still good.

Chapter 15

And in the End

THERE IS A GREAT difference between knowledge and wisdom. Knowledge derives from books and resides in the head; wisdom may include knowledge, but it is derived from life and resides in the heart or *kishkes*. For many years, I had labored at obtaining knowledge and in this I was very successful. But when it comes to wisdom, I am a slow learner.

When Judith Sanderson, a former colleague at Seattle University, encouraged me to take "leap of faith" and to affirm what I had only tentatively written, I came to realize that, over the course of these eighteen years, I had gone from hypothesizing about the meaning of suffering and our relationship with God to actually being able to affirm quite a few things. Talk about a process theology![1]

I subtitled this book "An Experience-based Theological Journey" because I tried to root every chapter in lived experience. Based on my personal experience of tragedy—and those of many other people—I debunked and rejected many of the traditional explanations for suffering (at least to my own satisfaction) and concluded that what happens in life is largely a matter of chance. God does not play an active role either in the events of our personal lives or in history. Based on this empirical observation, I rejected the traditional

1. For an introduction to Jewish process theology, see Artson, *God of Becoming and Relationship*; Englander, "How Powerful is God?"; *Spitzer*, "Why We Need Process Theology"; and Lubarsky and Griffin, *Jewish Theology and Process Thought*.

concept of petitionary prayer, which is based on asking for God's intercession, and came to focus on expressing gratitude for what is, being present in the moment, and seeking self-transformation as alternate forms of prayer. From my experience of what I perceived to be the divine, and drawing on the mystical experiences of others, I deconstructed the traditional God-concept of the Abrahamic faiths and built something new based on the ineffable experience of divine mystery. Then, consequently, I viewed revelation as a human response to that mystery, one that is global in its expression and accessible to everyone. Our holy texts and our religions thus are human creations, best understood in their historical and cultural contexts down through the ages—which in no way diminishes their present spiritual value. Now, in this chapter, I return to the issue of alleviating suffering because, having taken God out of the equation, responding to suffering becomes a wholly (and holy) human task. Consequently, I explore how best to choose life and live life, both as individual human beings and collectively as one human family, together all other living creatures on this planet. And for me, it all begins with a leap of faith.

My Leap of Faith

My leap of faith is to affirm that what we do, how we act, somehow matters to YHVH, not in the personal way that traditional religions posit our behavior to be tallied by a father/judge God, but in some way nonetheless, because everything we do has far-reaching effects. And when I really listen to my gut, then I hold a fluttering hopeful sensation that YHVH may somehow participate in what happens here and that is for the better.

I do not believe this is mere wishful thinking. I know that YHVH is capable of being experienced *because I have experienced It.* From that singular experience, I maintained the sensation that I am / we are organically—spiritually, if you will—part of a greater Whole. Second, an equally important part of my formative spiritual experience was a profound sense of the "goodness" of creation. Not that everything is good—because clearly it is not—but good in the sense of life tending toward the positive and the fulfillment of its potential, and the beauty that exists in that process. When I remind myself that I have felt YHVH in this way, then I feel that life gains in significance because of this Presence. Life is good, it is a blessing—and this is what YHVH Is.

I wish I could definitively assert that, somehow and in some way, our constructive deeds actually enhance YHVH's presence in our world and that our negative actions somehow actually diminish YHVH's presence as well, but I cannot jump quite this far. What I can say for certain is that *our sense* of YHVH's presence in the world is affected by how we act. When our sense of God's presence and the good that exists in our society is incrementally weakened by ripples of increasingly negative behavior it becomes, in Martin Buber's phrase, a time of the eclipse of God. Conversely, when people respond to the needs of unknown others in times of natural disasters, or when people respond appropriately to political atrocities, or when we respond one-on-one to another person in need, then I feel *as though* God's presence is being built up and that, in turn, we are strengthened and encouraged by that activity. Regardless of what happens on God's end, it is definite that people are strengthened and encouraged by the positive activity of other people (and similarly influenced by negative behaviors).

I like to imagine that there is a scale balancing good and evil in this world and that human behavior affects this balance. When the two are in balance, then goodness flows naturally into the world because Creation is basically good, and life is a blessing. And, if ever more people do good—who knows?—it might herald a messianic age (for a while).

And how do we get there? By increasing our trust in one another. To do so, there is a second leap of faith that I must take—that we all might take—and that is to dare to trust ourselves and one another to be reliable and compassionate, even if this runs counter to historical or personal experience. Trust is a psychological process, a spiritually transformative experience, and a personal commitment to our individual and collective potential to build a growing force for good in the world. To take this leap of faith and to truly trust other human beings is to begin the process of redemption because it nurtures a sense of hope. For some people, this long jump goes even further, extending to the belief—or having faith—that God actively cares for us as individuals, for humanity, and all Creation. Bravo to those who can take this extra leap—but, as for me, my head informs me that trust in God and humanity is unwarranted while my heart implores me both to trust and to be trustworthy, nonetheless. So, leap I must, to vault over my fears and dare to trust.

The Choice Before Us

In the book of Dvarim/Deuteronomy, Moshe lays before the Children of Yisrael—and by extension, all of us—a loaded choice of momentous proportions: God offers us both "life" or "death"; "blessing" or "curse"; "good" or "bad."[2] God, we are told, wants us to choose the good—life and blessing, not death and curse—and invites us to follow the commandments or face dire consequences. (*This is a choice?!*)

In all the Abrahamic faiths, the traditional "God" certainly is not above using fear and threats to manipulate humanity into doing good. Today, however, we can choose to think differently; we can choose "life" and "blessing" without fear. Marianne Williamson, in her book *A Return to Love*,[3] suggests that we have internalized senses of fear and love, the consequences of which appear as "blessings" and "curses" in our world. She identifies fear as "our shared lovelessness" and sees its expression in a host of evils including selfishness, greed, addiction, abuse, and war. Love, on the other hand, is expressed and experienced as lovingkindness, mercifulness, compassion, joyfulness, and so on. We can choose, with every action, whether to "extend love" or "extend fear"—the blessing or the curse.

Love means standing together, hoping together, building together. Love builds even when life's experiences may destroy.

---

2. Dvarim/Deuteromony 30:15; 19. The latter pair is often translated as "prosperity" and "adversity."

3. Williamson, *Return to Love*, xxi–xxii; 17–26 *et passim*.

Through love, we can defy, delay, and, for a time, even reverse this process of entropy. We need to capture whatever joy happens to exist, be grateful for it, magnify it, and use it to conquer the looming despair that so often accompanies the random misfortunes of illness, suffering, and death. This defiant joy, this hope against hope, and the grateful sharing of little things, makes life more bearable, because the suffering is tempered, counterbalanced, and sometimes even displaced by the positive feelings being shared.

Simply put, our task is to learn how to show love to one another. Love is what makes of life a blessing. To love and be loved are the greatest gifts we can give and receive. It is how we choose to affirm life.

What is Required of Us

How do we love? According to Jewish teaching, we have free will to choose how we act, and God, as it were, encourages us along the right path by giving us the commandments, all centering around the idea that we should emulate God in our behavior (at least when God is on His best behavior).[4]

And what constitutes this model behavior? In God's purported Self-disclosure to Moshe on Mt. Sinai, God uses these words of Self-characterization: "YHVH, YHVH (the LORD, the LORD), a God merciful and gracious, slow to anger, abounding in lovingkindness and faithfulness, extending lovingkindness to the thousandth generation, forgiving iniquity, transgression, and sin."[5] Known as

4. As in "Be holy, for I, YHVH your God, am holy" (Vayikra/Leviticus 19:2). The chapter from which this verse is taken, called the Holiness Code, contains many examples about what in Judaism it means to be holy and to emulate God.

5. *Shemot/Exodus* 34:6-7. This is as close as Torah comes to describing/limiting God and it is used frequently in the Tanakh: *Bamidbar/Numbers* 14:18-19; *Yoel/Joel* 2:13; *Yonah/Jonah* 4:2; *Michah/Micah* 7:18; *Tehillim/Psalms* 86:15, 103:8, 145:8; *Nehemyah/Nehemiah* 9:17,31; *Divrei Hayamim Two/ Second Chronicles* 30:9. Ultimately, what is shown to Moshe on Sinai is little different in content than what he had been told at the start of his career. Then he was told, "I am who/what I am"; now he is told, "I will be gracious to whom I am gracious." Poor Moshe! In both cases, the circular answer Moshe receives

the Thirteen Attributes of Mercy, this phrase serves as the basis for divine forgiveness in Judaism and Jews quote these words back to God as a divine reminder in Jewish worship, most significantly on Yom Kippur (the Day of Atonement). Not surprisingly, the rabbis chose not to include the second part of the divine pronouncement, which dwells on God's punitive side.

It is likewise all too easy for us to be judgmental and unforgiving and punitive; the challenge for us—as apparently for God—resides in being loving and understanding. It is no sin to err on the side of compassion. This is a principle that applies just as surely to relations between human beings and nations as it does to God's relationship with us. It is precisely when we act compassionately and lovingly that we are fulfilling the commandment "to be holy like God is holy."

But what does "being holy" or "showing lovingkindness" entail? A *midrash* records a "debate" between rabbis of different generations about the greatest principle in the Torah.[6] Rabbi Akiva said that 'You shall love your neighbor as yourself' is the greatest principle in the Torah; but Shimon ben Azzai said that the sentence 'This is the book of the generations of man' is even greater because it points to the unity of humankind being created in the image of the divine. Rabbi Tanhuma, a third participant, taught that one should not interpret "Love your neighbor as yourself" to mean that if you despise yourself, you may also treat your neighbor similarly. Just the opposite: he is and will always be a being made in the image of God. For this same reason, my teacher, the late Arthur Lagawier, translated the verse as "Love your neighbor. S/he is like you."[7] Translating it this way, he thought, stressed the point that all human beings are endowed with equal, inalienable worth and should be treated with love accordingly.

---

shows that YHVH will not be limited; that although YHVH's qualities may be tasted, YHVH is ultimately unknowable.

6. *Sifra* 89b and *Bereisheet Rabbah* 24:7. Likewise, Jesus in *Matthew* 22:36-40 and *Mark* 12:29-31.

7. The Hebrew word "*kamocha*" is usually translated "as yourself" but he chose to translate it also correctly as "s/he is like you."

How to Live Love

Living love is what I think every faith ideally is all about. For example, at Multifaith Works, I saw many people acting on the most noble beliefs and values of their respective faiths to help people with AIDS in need of housing, care, emotional and spiritual support. The motivating factors were particular to each faith, but the resultant behavior was identical!

The Golden Rule is perhaps the only universal commandment humanity has. It is not a difficult commandment to remember— "Do unto others as you would have others do unto you"; "What is hateful to you, do not do to another"—although it is more difficult to practice than to preach. One scholar has noted that the Golden Rule focuses on oneself and one's own needs first. Instead, he proposes: "Do unto others as *they* would have you do unto them" because we first are required to enter into a relationship with the other person and understand that person's needs before acting.[8] His is an important clarification, but however one expresses it, the important thing is to live your version of the Golden Rule because the future of humanity depends on it.[9]

The prophet Hosheiya (Hosea) has God declare, "I will espouse you with righteousness (*tsedek*) and justice (*mishpat*), and with lovingkindness (*hesed*) and compassion (*rahamim*), and I will espouse you with faithfulness (*emunah*)."[10] These values—righteousness, justice, lovingkindness, compassion, and faithfulness—are the ways we express love in the world when we seek to emulate God. Although all are intertwined, I think that "*hesed*" is most important for the topic at hand. *Hesed* has overtones and hints of mercy, compassion, favor, faithfulness, goodness, piety, benevolence, righteousness, and graciousness. It is often translated as "steadfast love," but I prefer to translate it as "lovingkindness."

8. Schulz, TedxYork talk, April 22, 2015.

9. Consider Karen Armstrong's warning delivered at her TED talk in July 2009: "If we don't manage to implement the Golden Rule globally so that we treat all people as though they are as important as ourselves, I doubt we'll have a viable world to hand on to the next generation."

10. *Hosheiya/Hosea* 2:21-22.

From *hesed* come *gemilut hasadim*, acts of lovingkindness. So important is the practice of lovingkindness that one sage, Shimon the Just, taught that the world is sustained by three things: by (the study of) Torah, by worship, and by deeds of lovingkindness,[11] and Rav Huna, a later sage, taught that a person who studied Torah but did no deeds of lovingkindness was like one who had no God.[12] *Hesed* is the crucial Jewish principle for living a holy and good life, and deeds of lovingkindness are quintessential, demonstrable acts of Jewish piety and the desire to be godly or holy.[13]

Doing *hesed*, lovingkindness, has a positive ripple effect. When we choose to take positive, constructive actions in our own lives and in the lives of others, we are focusing our energies on the life-affirming blessings that come from choosing to do good. In Jewish tradition, we have a saying: "One *mitzvah* (commandment or good deed) leads to another"—good deeds work like infinite ripples in a pond, spreading outwards, influencing others. (Bad deeds also work in the same way.) Through caring relationships, we nurture those qualities in us that motivated our good deeds in the first place and this, in turn, encourages us to continue on the path of *hesed*. Ideally it will also inspire the recipient of *hesed* to act similarly to another person too, paying that initial good deed forward. Every one of our actions ripples out with infinite consequences.

I believe that, like the Golden rule, the concept of lovingkindness is universal; it is only articulated differently. What in the Jewish tradition is called *hesed* is analogous to the concepts of *agape* and

11. *Pirkei Avot* 1.2

12. *Babylonian Talmud*, Avodah Zarah 17b

13. Under the traditional conception of God, the motivation to follow God's will derived from a mixture of love, fear, and awe. To this, the rabbis added a reward or punishment system focused on the World-to-Come. For me, the matter is best framed thusly: Do the commandments, *however observed*, add holiness to the life of the individual and enhance a person's relationships with other human beings and with God? *If* they impart value and direction to everyday life, *if* they assist in dealing with life's transitions, *if* they help awaken a sense of wonder to the mystery of creation and to YHVH's presence in it, *if* they nurture a feeling of profound gratitude, and *if* they contribute to improving the world—*then* they are as important and as valid *as if* they had come directly from the mouth of God.

caritas in Christianity, to *rakhma* in Islam, to *karuna* in Buddhism, to *ren* and *de* in the Chinese Confucian and Daoist traditions, and to *daya* in Hinduism. This is the closest thing we have to a universal human religious value. It is religion at its best.

Whether we are responding to the needs of a loved one or an unknown individual or an entire people, there are few things we do that are as noble as caring for other people. The Rev. Gwen Beighle called this sort of activity a "ministry of presence" and saw its task as, not to console with theology or prayer, but simply to be present with the other person.

A nurse's practical yet compassionate care, a doctor's humane concern, a relative's hug, or friend's gentle touch or kind word all potentially have great impact because they can break through the wall of isolation that suffering builds. The same holds true if we get involved in the humanitarian issues of our day. When we dare to act with lovingkindness, we are making a real difference because God, as it were, has no other hands than ours with which to care for and comfort people in need.[14]

I want to acknowledge that, for many of us, however, it is easier to care for people from afar than it is to do so personally. Many people seem to fear encountering people who are sick and those in mourning, let alone actually wading into a humanitarian crisis. Experiences like these make most of us anxious and uncomfortable, me included. Perhaps it is instinctive, perhaps it is superstitious; I don't know. Even with training, it is emotionally and spiritually challenging to be present in such settings. In situations like these, it is always important to remember that the people who are suffering are at the center of the crisis, not us; that they need us to be there, to stand with them, to listen to them, to celebrate the little joys, and to surround them with compassion.

Empathize with others. Practice your way of compassion. Help your fellow human beings, whomsoever they are and wherever they

---

14. The phrase is Dorothee Soelle's. She has observed: "God has no other hands than ours. If the sick are to be healed, it is our hands that will heal them. If the lonely and the frightened are to be comforted, it is our embrace, not God's, that will comfort them."

may live.[15] And when we assist other people, when we act with lov-ingkindness, when we show love to one another, I like to think, I hope, and almost believe that we are helping to build up YHVH's presence in the world.

When we follow the way of *hesed*, or *agape*, *karuna*, and so on, we consciously overcome the separateness and isolation that is bred in each of us. True, we can never surmount life's natural barriers, but by acting in a selfishly selfless way (for that is what the Golden Rule teaches) we are somewhat able to transcend that which separates one from another. Practicing lovingkindness is the best we can offer our fellow creatures, both human and beast, and the rest of creation. It builds bonds of connection; of unity, love, and trust; and enables us to repair our world.[16] This same principle of noble cooperation can apply to almost every issue confronting humanity today from environmental degradation to alleviating poverty and disease to resolving conflicts. The work transcends every faith tradition and every culture; it belongs to all of us yet exclusively to none of us.

I look for "God's presence" in an open heart, being demon-strated in deeds of caring for one another in daily life and cel-ebrated in joy and gratefulness. I look for "God" in how we raise our children and how we treat our fellow human beings and other living creatures. Do we treat them with honor and respect, or do we shame them, judge them, punish them? I look for "God" in whether we help others dealing with despair and suffering, in whether we create hope and spread joy. Ideally, what one believes reinforces one's practice of lovingkindness.

Living in this way means to have hope for the future despite experience and regardless of one's doubts about the goodness of ei-ther (or both) God and humankind. It means to have faith that, by doing acts of lovingkindness, others will be nurtured to do likewise

15. Isabel Wilkerson calls upon us to practice "radical empathy" which, for her (and me), means standing with oppressed people, past and present. See her book *Caste*, 386.

16. For extended meditations on lovingkindness and its place in our lives, see Fox, *Spirituality Named Compassion* and Armstrong, *Twelve Steps to a Compassionate Life*.

so that, trusting one another, together we may heal our world. Ripples of good extending ever-outwards beginning with one simple choice.

Choose life. . .

Chapter 16

A Personal Epilogue

I HAVE NOW COMPLETED over seventy-two earth orbits and, besides feeling a little dizzy at their apparent ever-increasing velocity, I feel it is time for some reflections.

Seventy years is the start date of the planned obsolescence of the human body, as is stated in *Tehillim/Psalm* 90:10 "The span of our life is seventy years, or, given the strength, eighty years." But I can tell you that my body started failing well before its warranty ran out. I've had a hip replacement and a double hernia operation, my prostate is enlarged, I have glasses and hearing aids, an essential tremor (I'd prefer non-essential, thank you), and I have arthritic thumbs, bad shoulders, and a bum knee. In short, I'm usually stiff in all the wrong places. . .

By my calculation, I have urinated approximately 184,000 times (based on 7 pisses/day x 365 days/year x 72 years), defecated at least 40,000 times (1.5 shits/day x 365 days/year x 72 years) and put food down my gullet more times than is possible to count. These pipes are getting old but, *danken got*, so far everything in this regard remains in working order!

So: I'm relatively healthy and still have more than half my wits about me. I've helped to grow a wonderful family that now includes two living daughters, three sons-in-law, and five grandkids. I love them all and I'm most fortunate to have found love again in the person of Richelle, my wife. Although my family and I have weathered some very challenging years, nonetheless I feel blessed by what I have in my relationships with family and friends.

As a Jew, I have endeavored to live my life according to God's own purported words concerning Avraham's descendants: "to keep the way of YHVH by doing what is just and right." To that end, I have observed the *mitzvot* in ways that are personally meaningful and helpful in keeping me spiritually focused on staying connected with the One, YHVH.

My career has been diverse and mostly meaningful, but I realize that the books and articles I've written will be my primary work legacy—and my efforts on behalf of the Kaifeng Jews and in the interfaith arena. Through my interpersonal relationships and interactions, my various jobs and my volunteer work, and my writings, I feel that in my own small way I will leave this world a little better—at least temporarily.

I recall the words of a samurai in some movie I saw many years ago: "Today is a good day to die." That is exactly how I feel at my age. For me, any day now is a good day to die—just spare me the pains of dying.

To be sure, there are many things I still want to do, and many experiences I still wish to have, and many relationships I continue to hold dear, but that bucket list is never empty. (Or maybe it's always being filled.)

There will always be more food to eat, more piss to pass, more shits to be shat, more sex to have, more stuff to read and walks to take, more occasions to commemorate, more love to share, more relationships to deepen, more people to help, more causes to champion, and more places to visit.

But I realize that life is just like that: there is always more to it. By and large, I've done just about the best I could with my life, and I am content. I am ready.

Death: the final frontier. To boldly go where everyone before has gone.

You, whom I will leave behind, whenever death comes to me, be happy for me—and may the memory of me be for a blessing.

Bibliography

Admirand, Peter. *Amidst Mass Atrocity and the Rubble of Theology: Searching for a Viable Theodicy.* Eugene, OR: Cascade, 2012.

———, ed. *Loss and Hope: Global, Interreligious and Interdisciplinary Perspectives.* London: Bloomsbury, 2014.

Agler, Richard. *The Tragedy Test: Making Sense of Life-Changing Loss: A Rabbi's Journey.* Eugene, OR: Resource Publications, 2018.

Agler, Richard, and Rifat Sonsino, eds. *A God We Can Believe In.* Eugene, OR: Wipf & Stock, 2022.

Aiken, Lisa. *Why Me, God? A Jewish Guide for Coping with Suffering.* Northvale, NJ: Jason Aronson, 1996.

Allender, Dan B., and Tremper Longman III. *Cry of the Soul: How Our Emotions Reveal Our Deepest Questions About God.* Colorado Springs, CO: NavPress, 1994.

Armstrong, Karen. *Twelve Steps to a Compassionate Life.* New York: Anchor, 2011.

Artson, Shavit. *God of Becoming and Relationship: The Dynamic Nature of Process Theology.* Woodstock, VT: Jewish Lights, 2013.

Bass, Diana Butler. *Grounded: Finding God in the World: A Spiritual Revolution.* New York: HarperOne, 2015.

Billman, Kathleen, and Daniel Migliore. *Rachel's Cry: Prayer of Lament and Rebirth of Hope.* Cleveland: United Church, 1999.

Birnbaum, David. *God and Evil: A Unified Theodicy/Theology/Philosophy.* Hoboken: KTAV, 1989.

Blumenthal, David R. *Facing the Abusing God: A Theology of Protest.* Louisville, KY: Westminster John Knox, 1993.

Borg, Marcus. *The God We Never Knew: Beyond Dogmatic Religion to a More Authentic Contemporary Faith.* New York: HarperCollins, 1997.

Boteach, Shmuley. *Wrestling with the Divine: A Jewish Response to Suffering.* Northvale, NJ: Jason Aronson, 1995.

Bowler, Kate. *Everything Happens for a Reason.* New York: Random House, 2018.

Braiterman, Zachary. *(God) After Auschwitz: Tradition and Change in Post-Holocaust Jewish Thought.* Princeton, NJ: Princeton University Press 1998.

Brenner, Reeve R. *The Faith and Doubt of Holocaust Survivors.* Northvale, NJ: Jason Aronson, 1997.

Cosgrove, Elliot J., ed. *Jewish Theology in our Time: A New Generation Explores the Foundations and Future of Jewish Belief.* Woodstock, VT: Jewish Lights, 2013.

Dawkins, Richard. *The God Delusion.* New York: Houghton Mifflin, 2008.

Ehrman, Bart D. *God's Problem: How the Bible Fails to Answer Our Most Important Question—Why We Suffer.* New York: HarperOne, 2008.

Englander, Lawrence A. "How Powerful Is God? Lurianic Kabbalah and Process Thought." *CCAR Journal* (Fall 2007) 27–40.

Fishbane, Michael. *Sacred Attunement: A Jewish Theology.* Chicago: University of Chicago Press, 2008.

———. *Text and Texture: Close Readings of Selected Biblical Texts.* New York: Schocken: 1979.

Fowler, James W. *Stages of Faith: The Psychology of Human Development and the Quest for Meaning.* Rev. ed. New York: HarperOne, 1995.

Fox, Matthew. *A Spirituality Named Compassion: Uniting Mystical Awareness with Social Justice.* New York: Harper & Row, 1990.

Gibson, John W., and Judy Pigott. *Personal Safety Nets.* Seattle: Classic Day, 2007.

Green, Arthur. *Ehyeh: A Kabbalah for Tomorrow.* Woodstock, VT: Jewish Lights, 2003.

———. *Radical Judaism: Rethinking God and Tradition.* New Haven: Yale University Press, 2010.

———. *Seek My Face, Speak My Name.* Northvale, NJ: Jason Aronson, 1992.

Greenberg, Irving Yitz. *Cloud of Smoke, Pillar of Fire.* New York: National Jewish Resource Center, 1974.

Griffin, David. *God, Power, and Evil: A Process Theodicy.* Louisville: Westminster John Knox, 2004.

Harris, Sam. *The End of Faith: Religion, Terror, and the Future of Reason.* New York: Norton, 2004.

Heller, Joseph. *God Knows.* New York: Dell, 1984.

Heschel, Susannah, ed. *Abraham Joshua Heschel: Essential Writings.* Maryknoll, NY: Orbis, 2011.

Hitchens, Christopher. *God Is Not Great: How Religion Poisons Everything.* New York: Twelve, 2007.

Howe, Irving, et al. *The Penguin Book of Modern Yiddish Verse.* New York: Penguin, 1987.

Jacobs, Steven L. *Rethinking Jewish Faith: The Child of a Survivor Responds.* Albany, NY: State University of New York Press, 1994.

Jonas, Hans. "The Concept of God After Auschwitz." In *Out of the Whirlwind: A Reader of Holocaust Literature,* edited by Albert Friedlander, 465–76. New York: Schocken, 1976.

Katz, Steven, et al., eds. *Wrestling with God: Jewish Theological Responses During and After the Holocaust.* New York: Oxford University Press, 2007.

Kolitz, Zvi, ed. *Yossel Rakover Speaks to God: Holocaust Challenges to Religious Faith.* Hoboken: KTAV, 1995.

Kraemer, David. *Responses to Suffering in Rabbinic Literature.* New York: Oxford University Press, 1995.

Kushner, Harold. *Why Bad Things Happen to Good People.* New York: Avon, 1981.

Larson, Dale G. *The Helper's Journey: Working with People Facing Grief, Loss, and Life-Threatening Illness.* Champaign, IL: Research Press, 1999.

Laytner, Anson. *Arguing with God: A Jewish Tradition,* Northvale, NJ: Jason Aronson, 1990.

——. *The Mystery of Suffering and the Meaning of God: Autobiographical and Theological Reflections.* Eugene, OR: Resource Publications, 2019.

Laytner, Anson, and Jordan Paper. eds. *The Chinese Jews of Kaifeng: A Millennium of Adaptation and Endurance,* Lanham, MD: Lexington, 2017.

Lepore, Jill. "The Commandments: The Constitution and Its Worshippers." *The New Yorker,* January 17, 2011, 70–76.

Lubarsky, Sandra, and David Ray Griffin, eds. *Jewish Theology and Process Thought,* Albany, NY, State University of New York Press, 1996.

Mackenzie, Don, et al. *Getting to the Heart of Interfaith: The Eye-Opening, Hope-Filled Friendship of a Pastor, a Rabbi and a Sheikh.* Woodstock, VT, Skylight Paths, 2009.

——. *Religion Gone Astray: What We Found at the Heart of Interfaith.* Woodstock, VT: Skylight Paths, 2011.

Michaelson, Jay. *Everything is God The Radical Path of Nondual Judaism.* Boston: Trumpeter, 2009.

——. "The Floods in Mississippi: Punishment from an Angry God?" *Forward,* June 3, 2011.

Miles, Jack. *God: A Biography.* New York: Random House, 1995.

Morrow, William. *Protest Against God: The Eclipse of a Biblical Tradition.* Sheffield: Sheffield Phoenix, 2007.

Neeld, Elizabeth Harper. *Seven Choices: Finding Daylight After Loss Shatters Your World.* New York: Grand Central, 2003.

——. *Tough Transitions: Navigating Your Way Through Difficult Times.* New York: Warner, 2005.

Oord, Thomas J. *God Can't: How to Believe in God and Love after Tragedy, Abuse, and Other Evils.* SacraSage, 2019.

Paper, Jordan. *The Mystic Experience: A Descriptive and Comparative Analysis.* Albany, NY: State University of New York, 2004.

——. *The Theology of the Chinese Jews, 1000–1850.* Waterloo, ON: Wilfrid Laurier University Press, 2012.

Patt-Shamir, Galia. *To Broaden the Way: A Confucian-Jewish Dialogue.* Lanham, MD: Lexington, 2006.

Petuchowski, Jakob J. *Theology and Poetry: Studies in the Medieval Piyyut.* London: Routledge & Kegan Paul, 1978.

Pollak, Michael. *Mandarins, Jews, and Missionaries: The Jewish Experience in the Chinese Empire.* New York: Weatherhill, 1998.

Rubenstein, Richard L. *After Auschwitz: Radical Theology and Contemporary Judaism.* Indianapolis: Bobbs-Merrill, 1978.

Sacks, Jonathan. *Not in God's Name: Confronting Religious Violence.* New York: Schocken, 2015.

Schulweis, Harold M. *For Those Who Can't Believe: Overcoming Obstacles to Faith.* New York: Harper Collins, 1994.

Schwartz, Howard, and Anthony Rudolf, eds. *Voices within the Ark: The Modern Jewish Poets.* New York: Avon, 1980.

Singer, Ellen, ed. *Paradigm Shift: From the Jewish Renewal Teachings of Reb Zalman Schachter-Shalomi.* Northvale, NJ: Jason Aronson, 1993.

Soloff, Rav. "My God." *CCAR Journal* 46 (1999) 56–66.

Sommer, Benjamin D. *Revelation and Authority: Sinai in Jewish Scripture and Tradition.* New Haven: Yale University Press, 2016.

Spitzer, Toba. "Why We Need Process Theology." *CCAR Journal* (Winter 2012) 84–95.

Spong, John Shelby. *Why Christianity Must Change or Die.* San Francisco: HarperSanFrancisco, 1998.

Steindl-Rast, David. *Common Sense Spirituality: The Essential Wisdom of David Steindl-Rast.* New York: Crossroad, 2008.

———. *Gratefulness, the Heart of Prayer: An Approach to Life in Fullness.* New York: Paulist Press, 1984.

Stern, Sholom. *When Words Fail: A Religious Response to Undeserved Hurt.* Northvale, NJ: Jason Aronson, 1999.

Swinton, John. *Raging with Compassion: Pastoral Responses to the Problem of Evil.* Grand Rapids, MI: Eerdmans, 2007.

Teasdale, Wayne. *The Mystic Heart: Discovering a Universal Spirituality in the World's Religions.* Novato, CA: New World, 2001.

Twain, Mark. *Letters from the Earth.* New York: Crest, 1963.

Viorst, Judith. *Necessary Losses: The Loves, Illusions, Dependencies and Impossible Expectations That All of Us Have to Give Up in Order to Grow.* New York: Fawcett Gold Medal, 1986.

Wade, Nicholas. *The Faith Instinct: How Religion Evolved and Why It Endures.* New York: Penguin, 2009.

Weiss, Dov. *Pious Irreverence: Confronting God in Rabbinic Judaism.* Philadelphia: University of Pennsylvania Press, 2017.

Wels-Schon, Greta. *Portrait of Yahweh as a Young God, or How to Get Along With a God You Don't Necessarily Like But Can't Help Loving.* New York: Holt Rinehard & Winston, 1968.

White, William Charles. *Chinese Jews.* 2nd ed. Toronto: University of Toronto Press, 1966.

Whitney, Barry. *What Are They Saying About God and Evil?* New York: Paulist, 1989.

Wilkerson, Isabel. *Caste: The Origins of Our Discontents.* New York: Random House, 2020.

Williamson, Marianne. *A Return to Love: Reflections on the Principles of A Course In Miracles.* New York: HarperCollins, 1992.

Winkler, Gershon, and Lakme Batya Elior. *The Place Where You Are Standing Is Holy: A Jewish Theology on Human Relationships.* Northvale, NJ: Jason Aronson, 1994.

Wood, James. "Holiday in Hellmouth: God May Be Dead, but the Question of Why He Permits Suffering Lives on." *New Yorker,* June 9 & 16, 2008.

Wright, Robert. *The Evolution of God.* New York: Little Brown, 2009.

www.ingramcontent.com/pod-product-compliance
Lightning Source LLC
Chambersburg PA
CBHW060312100426
42812CB00003B/754

*9 7 8 1 6 6 6 7 7 0 4 9 0 *